Richard Burton:
So Much, So Little

In memory of my mother
Elvira Stead
(1913-1990)

Richard Burton:
So Much, So Little

PETER STEAD

SEREN BOOKS

SEREN BOOKS is the book imprint of
Poetry Wales Press Ltd
Andmar House, Tondu Road, Bridgend,
Mid Glamorgan

British Library Cataloguing in Publication Data

Stead, Peter, *1943-*
Richard Burton: so much, so little.
I. Title
791.43028092

ISBN 1-85411-040-3

The publisher acknowledges the financial support of the
Welsh Arts Council

Front Cover: Hal in *Henry IV part I*
(Photograph by Angus McBean)

Typeset in Palatino
Printed and bound in Great Britain by
WBC Limited, Bridgend, Mid Glamorgan.

Acknowledgements

A general acknowledgement is due to the British Film Institute for its
unstinting efforts in providing both stills (5, 9, 10, 11, 17, 18) and copyright
information. Other acknowledgements are due to the Hulton Picture
Company (1, 2, 3, 4, 13, 16); The Kobal Collection (6, 8) with Syndication
International (15); Turner Entertainment Co. (10: © 1964 Turner Entertainment Co. All rights reserved); Mr Pulman of Clydach Antiques for
his previously unpublished photograph (14); The Estate of Angus
McBean (7 and front cover). The front cover photograph was provided
by the Shakespeare Birthplace Trust.

Contents

Illustrations

1. In Port Talbot, 1953
2. *Hamlet*, Old Vic, 1953
3. Laurence Olivier
4. John Barrymore
5. Stanley Baker
6. *Hamlet*, New York, 1964
7. *Coriolanus*, 1952
8. *The Last Days of Dolwyn*
9. *Look Back in Anger*
10. *The Night of the Iguana*
11. *The Spy Who Came In From the Cold*
12. *Where Eagles Dare*
13. Taking a tutorial at Oxford
14. Visiting Cwmafan
15. Visiting London, 1971
16. *The Assassination of Trotsky*
17. *Wagner*
18. *Absolution*

Introduction

This study of Richard Burton is offered in four instalments and those instalments reflect the way in which the actor and the man came across to me over a period of thirty years. As a schoolboy I heard about his great exploits in Stratford and London and yet this distinction seemed to be contradicted by his rather indifferent films that regularly arrived at my local cinema. There was never any danger of him rivalling my American heroes such as Gregory Peck and Burt Lancaster. Later as a student one was positively embarrassed by his excesses and affectations especially when a connection with Wales was stressed. Finally the historian that I had become could see far more clearly why it was that the Wales of the Depression era had nurtured such a talent and why it was too that the English stage had been so grateful to receive it. The London of the early 1950s was obviously quite crucial to any understanding of the Burton phenomenon. First and foremost one needed to determine precisely why the young Welsh actor had occasioned so much excitement. Only then could one turn to the more complex question of which aspects of his own personality and of the British cultural scene allowed him so decisively to break away from the London stage, the only place where his talent had any real meaning.

As a schoolboy I had gone to Stratford to see Michael Redgrave's Hamlet and Laurence Olivier's Coriolanus and from that time I was hooked on Shakespeare in performance and intrigued by the question of what constituted great acting. Nevertheless it has taken several decades for me to realise quite how much I wanted to write about the place of acting in English-language cultures. I had thought of myself as a labour historian but then my friends Nicholas Pronay, Dai Smith and Jeffrey Richards urged me to combine my interests in social history and the cinema. I started to

7

write about the working class and film it was Poetry Wales Press
(now Seren Books) who urged me to comment on the depiction of
Wales on film and then saw that the time had come for me to
consider the stage and screen career of the best known Welshman
of the twentieth century.

My judgement on Richard Burton was shaped by a reading of
those many contemporary critics that he so obviously intrigued
and by long discussions with friends to whom I am deeply indebted. The Dylan Thomas Society, the Port Talbot History Society
and the Swansea University History Seminar all invited me to talk
about Burton and at these sessions it was I who learnt most. My
work was greatly facilitated by staff at the British Film Institute
Library, the Hulton and Kobal Picture Archives, the Boston Public
Library and especially the New York Public Library at Lincoln
Center where at a particularly busy time I was shown a good deal
of material and given a private viewing of Burton's filmed *Hamlet*.
Research was carried out whilst I was a Fulbright Scholar-in-
Residence at the University of North Carolina at Wilmington and
I will always be grateful to Bob Toplin, Melton McLaurin and
Bruce Kinzer for making that possible.

The highlight of this whole venture was an afternoon I spent
sipping sherry with Philip Burton at his lovely Key West home:
we were surrounded by portraits of the actor who had been his
ward. I am especially indebted to Graham Jenkins, Andreas
Teuber, Greg Mullavey, Tom Cripps, Robert Preyer and Gilbert
Bennett. As always my wife Elizabeth was a tremendous inspira-
tion although it must be said that she was far less susceptible to
the Burton charm than her Welsh husband. Our debates became
neatly focused on that observation of the Cardiff-reared impresario 'Binkie' Beaumont in which he pointed out that while nature
had given Burton 'so much' it had also given him 'so little'.

I
Olivier's Heir

I
Olivier's Heir

The English rather take it for granted that Drama and Theatre occupy a special place within their artistic heritage and that within succeeding eras the general vitality of those traditions will clearly signify the sophistication and complexity of the national culture. In truth the precise role and value of Theatre has been extremely problematic and there have been long periods when the actual process of putting on plays has had very little connection either with the mass of the population or with what was best and significant in contemporary writing and thought. The great tradition had been set in the Elizabethan period when the country's greatest dramatist and poet had written for an audience that had been both aristocratic and popular. Thereafter English Theatre had become more a matter of middle-class and middle-brow entertainment with a commercial management neatly packaging wit, style and melodrama in accordance with the prevailing metropolitan taste. New writers came and went but nobody ever seriously challenged the supremacy of Shakespeare and as regular revivals of his great classics were staged so the mainspring of English Theatre became the exploitation by showmen of individual acting stars who would breathe new life into ancient texts. All too often theatre could seem just a matter of subcultural social routine but what audiences really longed for were those moments of genuine insight or of emotional thrill which they associated not so much with the text or the direction but rather with the great actors of the moment. This had been the case for a long period from the mid-eighteenth century down to the Edwardian years and it was to be true again in the 1920s as the influence of Shaw began to wane.

The most famous sentence of theatrical criticism that had ever been written in England was Samuel Coleridge's observation that to see Edmund Kean act was "like reading Shakespeare by flashes of lightning". Throughout the nineteenth century it had been the prospect of lightning sparked by charismatic acting that had really sustained both the metropolitan theatre and the tradition of touring companies. Once again in the 1920s it became clear that it was great acting rather than new writing that both excited the critics and guaranteed full houses. Historians have had no difficulty in identifying the re-emergence of what has been called an Actors' or a Stars' Theatre with the great success of Lilian Baylis's Old Vic Theatre which she had taken over in 1912 and which gradually between the wars became associated with all that was most exciting in terms of the discovery of talent. It is not so easy though to explain why the Old Vic should have played this role of putting stars very much to the fore. The original intention had been to build up a more intelligent audience than that which frequented the West End theatres but in time it was realised that there was nothing like the rave reports of a new acting talent to attract potential play-goers across the river to what was generally regarded as a remote theatre. In addition the reliance on outstanding performances rather lessened the need for expensive productions and it was always said that Miss Baylis's prayer was for good actors who were also cheap. To a degree then the Old Vic tradition had been created by somewhat fortuitous and old-fashioned commercial gimmickry but the rivalry with the world of films had played a part. The movie moguls had made the star system their very own and now in the new age of talking pictures they were indicating as never before the value of having the names of players above the titles of particular films. Perhaps subconsciously the promoters of serious theatre were being prompted into exploiting their own matinée idols.

The new age of English acting was really launched by the Old Vic's 1929 production of *Hamlet* in which the Prince was played by the astonishingly youthful John Gielgud. At that time the classical theatre was dominated by middle-aged stars but now

Gielgud inaugurated a period in which audiences would increasingly go to productions of Shakespeare expecting to be thrilled by younger braver actors with a greater physical and vocal range. Gielgud was twenty-five when he played Hamlet for Miss Baylis and now he was joined by other players like Ralph Richardson, Donald Wolfit, Wilfred Lawson, Peggy Ashcroft and Edith Evans, all of whom had grown up in an era when theatre had to compete with films and who were bound to consider in what respect live acting should differ from the more melodramatic fare offered by movie stars. Theatre had always thrived on the sheer capacity of star actors physically to thrill audiences but it was perhaps inevitable in the 1930s, a decade of movie glamour and yet social drabness, that play-goers would be rewarded by the emergence of a young talent capable of generating lightning to an extent greater than anybody since Kean who had died a century earlier.

Laurence Olivier first appeared at the Old Vic as Romeo in 1935 but it was only when at the age of thirty he played Hamlet that the English-speaking world's most knowledgeable and dedicated Shakespearean audience fully realised that a new superstar had emerged and that truly a new era had opened in which classical theatre was back at the very heart of the nation's artistic life. There was now a clutch of youngish actors whose co-operation and rivalry made every classical production an event both of social debate and intellectual analysis and yet the beauty of the situation was that this new theatrical era was dominated by one glamorous actor and his equally glamorous wife who both moved effortlessly between the West End and Hollywood and who imbued Shakespeare and the classics with all the style and sexuality that the movies had aroused. Olivier and Vivien Leigh between them transformed the position of London's theatreland by pulling it out of an almost suburban isolation and giving it a new international dominance as something that fed off and into the world of film. The standard repertoire had been given new life and a younger generation thronged to theatres in which their minds were stimulated by actors who were undoubtedly classical and yet who were as physically exciting as those in the movies.

Throughout the 1940s and into the 1950s Olivier dominated the London stage and in so doing he created a renewed interest in the whole role of acting within the English theatrical tradition. Soon critics were resurrecting the notion that there was a mantle of greatness that had belonged to Burbage, had passed on to Garrick, Kean and Irving and which now had been taken up by Olivier. There was much talk of greatness but hardly surprisingly there was also some difficulty in defining it. There was much recourse to the standard quotations in which Dr Johnson, Coleridge and above all Hazlitt had attempted to define the essential techniques but in general frustration prevailed as critics realised the extent to which great stage acting was indeed a form of "sculpting in snow" and that as the memory faded there was neither the language nor the critical framework fully to capture and retain the precise nature of the greatness that audiences had experienced. An appreciation of acting was very much back in fashion and perhaps it was inevitable that a critic would emerge whose interest was as much in the individuality of the players as in the nature of the production and who could use his own sense of style as a base for an understanding of what constituted theatrical presence and genius.

What Olivier had done for acting, Kenneth Tynan was now to do for criticism. Throughout the land there were educated newspaper readers who sensed that exciting things were happening in the theatre but what was needed was a critic who could fully convey the nature of the new acting and who could make it imperative for those who wanted to keep abreast of cultural change to read the theatre columns as well as the book and film reviews. From his earliest days of reviewing Tynan was determined to establish the secret of Olivier's immense theatrical presence by analysing the contribution made by voice, intelligence, physique and movement. Then as he summed up each new performance, Tynan tended again and again to resort to the notion of Olivier's essentially feline nature. The critic might well here have been building on phrases first used a century earlier by George Henry Lewes for whom Kean had possessed a "terrible" but "beautiful" feline quality with "the playfulness of a panther showing her claws". For Tynan Olivier was usually either a panther or a lion: in *Oedipus Rex* his "jungle movements" made him a "panther among doves". He was a panther in the sense that all his actions emanated both style and controlled power, there was a coming together of intelligence and motion, the actor possessed an inbuilt economy and tact which on one occasion suggested to Tynan that the very truth of the performance was that "the thing he is shall make him live". As readers read these judgements and tried to conjure up the man in their own minds they must have been left in no doubt that Olivier's impact in the theatre was essentially physical. They would have known from films that the besuited Olivier was a very handsome, debonair and just a little exotic leading man but here was Tynan suggesting that on the stage the actor had an even greater capacity physically to thrill. In later years Olivier would confess that his Hamlet owed a great deal to that of Jack Barrymore and that the essence of the latter's interpretation of the Prince had been that he had "put the balls back". That precisely was what Olivier had done in general to Shakespearean Theatre first in the drab days of the thirties and then in the austere forties. The London stage had met the challenge of the movies and had won through to new and younger audiences. It had done this not by discovering new writers nor by totally revolutionising staging but rather by injecting a new vitality into fairly conventional productions. There was a new intelligence at work but one which relied very greatly on both vocal and physical bravado. Theatre could thrill, theatre was sexy.

Expectations had been aroused both in terms of the role of play-going in the life of the capital and in the obligation of producers to find new acting talent. Olivier, Gielgud and Richardson had all been born Edwardians, they had made their first impact in the 1930s, their theatrical greatness was inevitably linked with the triumph of the national culture in the hour of wartime need and their knighthoods duly followed; it became Sir Ralph and Sir Laurence in 1947 and, surely through oversight, Sir John only in 1953. Once those 1947 knighthoods had confirmed middle-aged celebrity, critics and theatre-goers were on the look out for those new stars who would take up the mantle. Perhaps there were a few who just counted themselves lucky to have seen genius once or twice in their lifetime and who now anticipated a return to a more mundane normality, but such had been the renewed interest in the English acting tradition in the 1930s that the consensus almost willed the new talent into existence. For a while there was to be frustration, a prevailing view that the thrill was missing. In those years immediately after the War there was a growing feeling that life in Britain was dull and that in literature, music, film and art mediocrity was the norm rather than that sense of cultural experiment which some had expected the outbreak of peace to occasion. On the stage too when the established stars were not available, worthiness seemed to be the norm. It was a time in which names like Quayle, Redgrave, Clements, Helpmann and Tearle served as guarantees of quality but not necessarily of excitement. There were no Oliviers in that list but there was one possible contender and not surprisingly it was Tynan who identified him. Paul Scofield was only twenty-six when he played Hamlet at Stratford in 1948 and immediately Tynan spotted that he alone amongst English actors shared Olivier's gift of radiating power without having to go in search of it through mannerisms. With both actors audiences were never aware of intention only of presence. Scofield too was "an animal that prowled", one that was dangerous and quite unpredictable both in terms of voice and motion. That vital physical thrill was there for Tynan and he confidently predicted greatness but other critics were far from convinced and demanded a little more control. For T.C. Worsley, Scofield could "take the stage, but does not give the impression of knowing quite what to do with it when he has it". London was waiting for Olivier's heir but clearly it was not going to be an easy path for the youthful claimants.

Richard Burton was indubitably to be Laurence Olivier's true heir and his surprisingly short and yet much discussed career in London's West End can only be fully comprehended within this lineage. The scene had been set: a highly commercialised, much vaunted and widely reported theatrical culture was indeed waiting for "a prince", one who would combine intelligence with animal power and who could prove that, even in the absence of new writers and directors, classical theatre could be a cultural imperative at once superior to the cinema and more physically direct. For one who was to pass so quickly through the West End Burton's arrival there came in strangely delayed instalments. He had first played on a London stage in 1944 but effectively his metropolitan career was launched five years later by the impresario Binkie Beaumont, who had seen him at Oxford in *Measure For Measure* and who had then three years later and after some difficulty found him a supporting rôle in a star-studded production of

16

Christopher Fry's verse drama *The Lady's Not For Burning* which in 1949 struck many critics as the best play to have been written since the War. This tale, set in the Middle Ages, was the unlikely vehicle in which the twenty-four year old Burton was to make his impact and that impact was first and foremost a physical one. Beaumont was later to sum it up as "sheer star-magnetism, hypnosis at its crudest and fiercest". Like so many others he was always to enjoy recollecting that moment in the play when John Gielgud and Pamela Brown were talking front stage. Behind them Burton as the young boy was scrubbing the floor, scrupulously acting as directed, speaking his occasional lines quietly and yet "the audience ignored the two stars and looked only" at him, "watching him carefully wondering what he was going to do and say next".

Nobody seemed to resent this scene-stealing for it was generally appreciated that he was perfect for the part and that he had taken to it instinctively. "I never had to tell him anything at all, except not to yawn so much when he wanted his lunch" recalled Gielgud who was also directing. Expectation had been aroused but it was another two years before he accepted rôles in which he could make any impact. At Stratford in 1951 he played Prince Hal and fulfilled all the promise for which his admirers were longing. Again it was the power that radiated from his sheer stage presence that shaped the critical comment. Reactions were running along familiar lines: for Philip Hope Wallace "the eye picks him out and refuses to leave him" whilst for T.C. Worsley he had "that indefinable quality which draws the eyes of the audience exclusively towards him". For Tynan he was "a still brimming pool running disturbingly deep". Of all the judgements made on this new Shakespearean star, however, two stood out because of the way in which they drew attention to how appropriate it was that the action of the Fry play had called for Burton to mime the building of a cathedral. Their reactions to that aspect of the earlier play were always to be used to evoke the strangeness and even the essence of the young actor. It was the doyen of London critics Harold Hobson who thought that with this Hal the audience had been offered "a young knight keeping a long vigil in the cathedral of his own mind" whilst it was an acting colleague who gave Kenneth Tynan a quote that he was to make famous by suggesting that

17

when Burton came on stage he "brings his own cathedral with him".

In the guise of Hal a very handsome and striking new prince had indeed made his entry into the theatrical kingdom and clearly directors had at their disposal a new physical and possibly spiritual force. Burton's impact had been quite immediate and from that production of *Henry IV* onwards he was openly spoken of as what Worsley called "the coming actor" and as "the new Olivier". At the same time though the critics were tending to stress promise rather than achievement and their glowing phrases of praise were accompanied by many reservations. At the outset there was the straightforward point that he was better in some parts than in others; in that summer at Stratford it was generally accepted that he was less good as the mature king in *Henry V*. Some critics tended to forget that no actor could be perfect in every rôle but their disappointment was powerful testimony to how much that Hal has promised. More fundamental were the criticisms made of some of Burton's physical attributes and in this respect it was obvious that critics were having some difficulty in coming to terms with a very new kind of theatrical presence. Most people watch an actor's head and here at least there was only admiration and envy. Alec Guinness thought it was the head of a Roman emperor and Anthony Quayle spoke of Burton as having "the heaven-sent actor's mark" with wide-apart eyes and good cheekbones. Undoubtedly it was the head that conveyed dignity and authority but with other attributes there was far less consensus and even doubts whether he was suitable for classical roles. Even Binkie Beaumont who had so immediately reacted to his potential remembers the Burton he had seen at Oxford as having "a thick and clumsy body". Tynan was always aware of Burton's relative shortness and words like "stocky" and "compact" usually found their way into his reviews to indicate his nagging concern. Very rarely had critics mentioned Olivier's height and that was because his litheness made it irrelevant. Burton was a less mobile actor and so his apparent stockiness became a talking point. For Alan Dent he was only a "bantam" sized Henry lacking in physical stature and there were to be several references to the Prince with the coal-miner's legs or the rugby-player's body. Equally, and this has been largely forgotten, there were many reservations about the voice and this was surprising for Burton's training had been largely in the recital of verse and already he was creating a reputation as a fine radio actor. Tynan detected an element of rant in his Henry whilst P.L. Mannock thought that the voice was not used creatively, there were no sustained heroics and "the full music of spoken poetry" was lacking. That fine critic Audrey Williamson was to respond to Burton's "hard edge in the upper register" and his "blasting fortissimo" but also complained of the voice's monotony; there was no irony and therefore no subtlety. On several occasions T.C. Worsley was to comment on his faulty voice technique and the need for more intensive training and J.W. Lambert even went so far as to insist that his voice "let him down" for "it will not carry thunder but under pressure grows shrill". For the *Times* critic too Burton became inaudible when at full volume.

What all these reservations and qualifications indicate is that what the critics had detected was not so much a fully-rounded acting talent but rather a new and challenging theatrical power that needed to be more firmly channelled and controlled. Reading those early reviews one senses too the extent to which the critics were dealing with not so much an undeveloped talent as an alien one. Olivier had been physically exciting and disturbing but had always been essentially acceptable because his roots were known and were familiar. Certainly there had always been a touch of the exotic about him, something Huguenot or Latin, but in every other respect he was an out-and-out London suburbanite, a bourgeois, an Anglican (fashionably High no doubt) and perhaps just an exceptionally fine example of a type who would love to dress up and so inspire the theatrical set in any good school. By comparison, and that comparison was now commonplace, Burton was a stranger and the power that he radiated was all the more threatening because it was both physically and socially mysterious. For most critics it was a question of race and of temperament. Tynan so wanted to be impressed and was certain that he had found the new Olivier and yet he was worried that Burton's reserve and "rooted solitude which his Welsh blood tinges with mystery" were imposing limits on his acting range. For Caryl Brahms his acting was not sufficiently "sunny", not contagiously exciting enough to give him star personality and like that of Robert Helpmann had a "strange curdled quality". *The Times* too was to refer to a sullenness and a melancholy in his acting, whilst Worsley thought that early on he tended to rely far to heavily on a natural and youthful "sulky Welsh charm". Writing in the *New Statesman* Worsley was always to stress Burton's "star-personality", "extra-ordinary power" and "quiet command" but he also made it clear that more work was needed if the qualities of youth were to be converted into a sustained theatrical career. Burton was different and the critics could never quite reconcile themselves to the fact that Shakespearean power was being conveyed by such an out-sider. It was Worsley perhaps who so nicely encaptured the criti-cal dilemma for he was to find Burton's Hamlet very acceptable indeed; nevertheless he had to explain to his readers that "by his nature" the young actor did not possess qualities that were essen-tial for the part for "he cannot suggest the poet, nor the courtier, nor the scholar". Here very obviously was a new kind of Hamlet, a new kind of acting talent.

For some critics Burton was never to become the ideal Shakes-pearean actor but for his real supporters he was always getting better and better. Again it is in Worsley that we can most easily trace the way in which the vocal range was improved and in which tricks and mannerisms gave way to technique. With hindsight we can more readily appreciate how quickly Burton was learning his craft and how very early in his Shakespearean career some kind of mastery was achieved. There is a danger here that the sub-sequent debate on his personality might encourage us to pass over this period in his career without realising his full achievement. The notion was to develop that Burton was an actor lost to the stage and one lost at a point where he was beginning to look like Olivier's successor. Similarly the fact that his appeal rested on qualities over and above those of his acting skills is sometimes used to devalue what in fact he accomplished. From the start he had been identified as a sexual phenomenon, first perhaps by the homosexuals prominent in London production and then by a growing number of female colleagues and supporters. The gossip in the tabloid press and his growing popularity in New York and in Hollywood made it inevitable that his later seasons at the Old Vic would be a popular 'show-biz' event but we would be quite mistaken to conclude that his impact was due entirely to some kind of animal or sexual magnetism. His very striking Prince Hal had come at Stratford in the early summer of 1951; just two years later he was playing Hamlet at the Edinburgh Festival. As we have seen T.C. Worsley thought that was an impressive performance "although the control is not yet absolutely certain". That control however was far more in evidence a month later when the production opened at the Old Vic. In Edinbugh *Hamlet* had been played on an open platform stage but now on a smaller traditional stage and in an intimate theatre Worsley found that "a valiant attempt" had become "a sure achievement" in which the audience was carried "into the living and suffering centre of poetic tragedy". The *Times* also appreciated the transformation and explained that at Edinburgh there was power in the soliloquies but a curious lack of charm elsewhere whereas now there was a sustained charm which encompassed reserve, shock, tenderness, gaiety and anger. This was, concluded the critics of London's most prestigious newspaper, "as satisfying" a Hamlet "as any that memory can recall for a great many years". Five months later Burton was playing the title-role in *Coriolanus* and succeeding even more triumphantly than he had as Hamlet. This was a notoriously problematic role for actors and one in which the main character's general unattractiveness had made it difficult for either critics or audiences to respond with any enthusiasm. *The Times* found it a little hard to believe that a Coriolanus with as much charm as Burton's would ever have had so many problems with the Roman citizenry but in general the critic appreciated the actor's voice, presence and power especially in the scenes with his mother. For Worsley Burton offered "tremendous bravura" as the arrogant, patrician, professional soldier who lauds the efforts of his men as soldiers only to despise them as they later attempt to claim their political rights. This was the finest performance of the rôle Worsley had ever seen and that is a judgement that has become part of modern critical wisdom. Writing in 1988 the American scholar Garry Wills urged his readers to consider the play as one that "speaks directly and ominously to the politics of our times" and to note that Olivier and Burton had provided the two great modern versions. He gave thanks that Burton's performance as the "perpetually hurt and hurting warrior" had been preserved on record.

Within a period of just over two years Burton had displayed greatness in the rôles of Prince Hal, Hamlet and Coriolanus, and within the next year, during which time he and John Neville had become the popular heroes of the Old Vic's audience, he was to add a much improved Henry V and an impressive Iago to his list of triumphs. Given this record it is insulting to think of him as someone who might have developed into a kind of Olivier for in a sense he had already created a niche for himself alongside the older actor. It has taken recent biographers of Lord Olivier to remind us that many of his earlier performances received mixed reviews, that he did not succeed in every rôle, that unlike Gielgud he was not an instantly successful Hamlet, and that his all-round genius for Shakespearean acting was refined over a long period of time and sometimes by appearances in several versions of the leading roles. English audiences were undoubtedly hungry for a new talent to succeed Olivier and by 1956 there could be little doubt that they had been given precisely that. What was remark-able was not only Burton's rapid improvement and high success rate but also the way in which he had seemed to by-pass all the normal channels which fed talent onto the London stage. He was quite truly a stranger who had come from nowhere. He had not been trained at one of the established acting schools and neither had he served a long apprenticeship at one of the highly respected provincial repertory companies. Traditionally in England the stars of tomorrow can be seen coming along the pipeline, whereas with Burton it was more a question of tantalising glimpses amidst long mysterious absences. His West End debut had been in 1944 and although his great breakthrough in the Christopher Fry play came in 1949 and his Prince Hal in 1951 it can still be argued that he became a great Shakespearean actor with far less formal training than any of his rivals. He had been trained by his guardian, Philip Burton, as a verse-reader and as a radio actor and from this source had come constant guidance as to how the Shakespearean roles should be tackled. There had been some advice given during his six months at Oxford but the only real theatrical training had been on the road in Emlyn Williams' company. It was no wonder that in his early roles Burton was accused by critics of relying too heavily on his instinctive and natural charm and of direct imita-tion of Olivier, and neither was it surprising that he had to make so many adjustments during the time he was actually on the stage at Stratford and the Old Vic. Whatever a successful actors's natural advantages and inherent charm these things need to be supplemented if any kind of sustained exposure to national critical judgement is to be acceptable. Technique has to be learnt and it was that which Tynan, Worsley and his other supporters could see Burton aquiring rôle by rôle in that short time between 1951 and 1956.

It would be a mistake to imagine that Burton just walked off the street and into the rôle of Prince Hal for there had been many hours of work with his mentor and many hours of rehearsal for all his roles but the fact remains that he was considerably less well trained than nearly all other great contemporary Shakespearean actors. In recent years Simon Callow and Antony Sher have made us all far more aware of the rigour needed to develop acting skills to West End standards and earlier this had been the experience of Gielgud who had trained with Constance Benson, with Olivier who had been at the Central School and with Scofield who spent time at two theatre schools. All three actors had already been introduced to a number of techniques and to a range of parts before moving on to spend years in repertory companies where there was again an emphasis on allowing talented youngsters to discover their identity by playing in as many varied productions as contemporary taste could bear. It is interesting to compare Burton with that small group of great English stars whom he had come to rival, but in many ways his impact as a very handsome and physically impressive outsider prompts a more meaningful comparison with his almost exact contemporary Marlon Brando.

The American actor was a year and a half older than Burton and had been born in a Nebraska that was far more physically remote and culturally adrift from Broadway than was Port Talbot from London's West End. By the time he was nineteen Brando had drifted into New York City and then four years later had come his great theatrical breakthrough in the part of Stanley Kowalski in *A Streetcar Named Desire*. The Broadway audience exalted over the discovery of this new very physical actor who just exuded animal magnetism and raw sex appeal. They were not however looking at a farm boy who had wandered in from the prairie but rather an aspiring young actor who had alighted on a city where acting technique was being discussed and analysed more seriously than anywhere else in the world, and where his potential was spotted and developed first by the highly acclaimed instructor Stella Adler and then by the brilliantly inventive director Elia Kazan. The Marlon Brando that thrilled Broadway in 1947 and then the wider world of film-goers in 1950 represented the coming together of natural American beauty and quite considerable Manhattan know-how.

By contrast Richard Burton was an amateur and however much he was prompted by Philip Burton, Emlyn Williams and then by directors like John Gielgud, Anthony Quayle and Michael Benthall one senses that his Welsh charm was being augmented by his own instincts as much as by formal instruction. This matter of his lack of formal training clearly helps to explain many of the short- comings in his early performances but perhaps it was even more decisive than that, inasmuch as it allows us to understand why his classical English career was over so quickly. Everyone knows how John Neville and Burton alternated the parts of Othello and Iago and how in so doing they delighted the youngsters who had queued for long hours in the Waterloo Road but the absolutely astounding fact is that when Burton left that production in 1956 he had left the London stage for ever.

Over the years the various biographies of Burton had explained to us that he had never quite taken acting seriously and that he had some unease about it as a career but it was only with the publication of Melvyn Bragg's much fuller study in 1988 that we were able to appreciate the quite considerable contempt that he had for the profession. Working from casual comments made over the years and then from Burton's own diaries Bragg draws the picture of a man who felt guilty that he was "not doing real man's work", who was deeply uneasy at having to make up or to wear costumes or wigs, who was quickly bored with any part and who could only make a long run tolerable by varying his performance every night even to the extent of imitating other accents and other actors or later in his American career by drinking both before and during his time on stage. In short he never naturally regarded himself as an actor and this explains precisely how it was that he could so totally and finally distance himself from a theatrical world that was so eager to crown him as its king. It was clear at a very early stage that he approached the job with a remarkable detachment, confident in his own ability to succeed without reference to prevailing wisdom. Actors who are trained in schools are learning the skills of a profession but Burton in that sense was never a professional; actors who train in repertory begin to pride themselves on their versatility and ingenuity but he never needed that kind of satisfaction. Actors from all kinds of backgrounds are delighted to accept roles that help them to come to terms with their own personality — but he was never particularly in need of that kind of confirmation. Success had always come easily and naturally and that prompted the feeling that it would be foolish to disrupt the flow; similarly it suggested that it might be just as well to call it a day sooner rather than later. He had never doubted that it was his voice, his charm and his sex-appeal combined with his native intelligence that had taken him from Port Talbot to Stratford and the Old Vic, and it was obvious too that it was precisely the same qualities that guaranteed him personal friendships and love as well as respect and awe from beyond the footlights. His intelligence and physical robustness would see him through a part but nothing that had happened to Richard Burton for one moment suggested that he owed his success to any body of thought or corporate effort. He had arrived as a personality and not as a trainee actor and in almost everything they said the favourable critics were really confirming his own instincts. If you have your own cathedral you don't really need a wig and you certainly don't need six years in provincial rep. As Binkie Beaumont was later to confirm he was an actor who was confident that he had nothing to learn and that to attempt to submit talent to experiment and routine was to risk losing it.

That Burton was so widely acclaimed as a stage personality was as much a comment on his age as it was on his own sense of certainty. He had walked into a theatre culture in which the search for a new Olivier and the easy way in which critics could talk of a great acting tradition that stretched "from Burbage to Burton" had almost eclipsed any interest in contemporary drama. Shakespearean audiences at any time or in any place would be honoured by the combined talents of John Neville and Richard Burton but clearly their astonishing impact at the Old Vic was as much a comment on metropolitan culture as it was on their acting skills.

For some decades the old theatre had fought to outdo the cinema and now there was the added rivalry of a much improved and more varied television service. More than ever before there was logic in the tactics of star billing and of expropriating cinematic glamour, especially in an age when all kinds of groups in society were responding to affluence, to advertising and to American influences by developing new styles and fashions to replace an earlier austerity and suburban drabness. Neville and Burton were certainly the new Gielgud and Olivier but they were more than that for they had become the way by which classical theatre was reaching out to establish its credentials in a rapidly changing society that had no real need to accept existing social and cultural shibboleths. It was not entirely obvious that Neville was the son of a Willesden mechanic and Burton of a Welsh miner but none-theless there were many different kinds of people eager to claim these new stars as their special link with what was otherwise a traditional theatre. They were thirtyish and that made them young in a country that had just seen the retirement of an eighty year old prime minister. They were grammar school types and also ex-ser-vicemen and that made them very acceptable to a new generation of fledgling intellectuals who were coming to feel that it was time for people with this kind of background to lay claim to leadership in many walks of national life. It was a time too when tabloid and middle-brow newspapers were suddenly aware of how younger people were beginning to claim London as their own and how photographs of and gossip about personalities was becoming a hallmark of new life styles. The acting duo had become a sensation and they had become fashionable. Here was confirmation that London could be rescued from artistic mediocrity and at the same time rival Hollywood at its own game. The young were leading the acclaim but a new pattern was being set in which so many cultural fellow-travellers were eager to pick up the latest trend and this was as true of visiting dignitaries as it was of all those groups who wanted to believe that London was relevant. The Old Vic offered the best show in town. This was certainly Shakespeare lit by lightning and there centre stage as Henry V, Othello or Iago was an actor with whose face the audience was already intimately familiar, courtesy of Hollywood, and yet the man remained a mysterious outsider who came with all the exotic and yet elemental appeal of a solo jazz musician.

We now know that this could never be enough for Richard Burton. He loved the acclaim but both culturally and emotionally it did not really mean anything satisfactory. Similarly those thrills in the Waterloo Road could not be enough for English theatre and for the new generation of young intellectuals. A sea-change was about to occur and it was a sea-change with which the young Welsh actor was only ever to be marginally associated. His great successes had come in the last few years of a distinctive era in the history of theatre and in the history of popular culture. London was about to be transformed in a way with which Burton would never really catch up. People from very similar backgrounds to his, although perhaps just a little younger, were to claim as their own many aspects of British national life but none quite so spectacularly as the theatre. Suddenly, and at precisely the moment that Burton was going into exile, there was a new theatrical culture in London, one based in part on new experimental companies, like George Devine's English Stage established at the Royal Court in 1955 and Joan Littlewood's Theatre Workshop which had found a home at the Theatre Royal, Stratford East in 1953.

There were new writers too ensuring at last that not all the headlines were about Shakespearean revivals; there were the Irishmen Samuel Beckett and Brendan Behan, and three English dramatists, John Osborne, Harold Pinter and Joe Orton, all of whom had been repertory company actors and who had picked up a sure sense of what worked in the theatre as well as smouldering contempt for the deadness of what was throughout their native land a largely middle-class theatre. Alongside them were the new directors such as Peter Hall, William Gaskill and John Dexter who were equally in rebellion against the conventions of the West End and of provincial rep and who realised that the new drama of ideas and protest required that at last the English should catch up with well-established international notions of staging and acting. Finally in this new theatrical culture there were the new actors, men and women recruited now overwhelmingly from the provinces and from lower middle-class and working-class backgrounds, players who could come up with all the accents and passions to express the new anger required by the young playwrights just as they were able to give a new energy and contemporary feel to the startling new productions of the classics that the young directors were staging. Suddenly there was a whole new generation of acting talent led by Albert Finney, Richard Harris, Peter O'Toole, Tom Courtenay, Rachel Roberts and Joan Plowright, players who were to be famed at least initially for their naturalism, but all of whom had been scrupulously and rigorously trained in the leading acting academies.

If, as Bragg suggests, Richard Burton regarded acting as some kind of cosmic joke, then certainly the biggest joke in his own career was the way in which he missed out on this cultural revolution. He was just four years older than John Osborne, five years older than Peter Hall and Harold Pinter, and eleven years older than Albert Finney and yet in theatrical terms he was to belong to a previous era. It could well have been that Burton would always have wanted to be an outsider, someone who would do it all on his own and by using his own resources, but surely if he had been at a London acting school or a young actor looking for his first job his intelligence and ambition would have taken him towards the best and most exciting minds as they attempted to transform both the intellectual and social roles of drama? Of course he had always been guided and coached but he had never really been forced to come to terms with acting other than as a vehicle for his own charisma. His work was something he would do to prove that he could do it and for acclaim but it had never been part of any real intellectual or cultural context. His success was personal rather than a contribution to any national understanding of what theatre was about. The younger actors were to be as ambitious and perhaps as self-centred but they always had to share the headlines and the credit with the writers and directors and so critics and journalists were never to leave them in any doubt as to their precise place within the new debate on the national culture in which provincial anger and social mobility were key themes. Acting becomes something very different when it is being staged within a writers' or a directors' theatre and once again in this respect we are reminded of the contrast between Burton and Brando. The young Nebraskan had arrived in a city consumed by an interest in acting, but only as a vehicle for new writing and always within the framework of effective staging.

Tennessee Williams and Kazan had been waiting for their young man to appear whereas Burton had gone straight into Shakespeare and been hailed as the successor to a star who had first appeared in major roles in the 1930s. Burton then was just to miss out on the chance of becoming an actor within a cultural revolution, of becoming an agent of cultural change in the way that Brando and Finney were. This was a joke on him and it was to be a particularly savage one because very soon Sir Laurence Olivier himself realised that what had been identified as the New Wave was enriching rather than destroying the English stage. He decided to place himself firmly within the new movement and he did this by first requesting and then bringing alive John Osborne's character Archie Rice in *The Entertainer*, by marrying the Royal Court's leading actress and then by establishing a truly National Theatre, which was housed initially and very appropriately at the Old Vic and to which many of the younger writing, directing and acting talents were to be attracted.

In 1955 Richard Burton was undoubtedly theatreland's most exciting asset and most valuable commodity and yet he was at the point of going into a total and final exile. We can now fully appreciate the irony of those journalists who at that time were reminding audiences of how lucky they were in being able to see on stage a star who was being paid only a fraction of what he could earn in Hollywood. Here, according to one long-forgotten account was an actor whose "loyalty" to the "ardour and endurances of the Old Vic and of the great Shakespearean roles" was proof indeed that "drama was not doomed". Well drama was not doomed, far from it, but Burton's contribution to it certainly was. His career was to touch the new realist wave at two points both courtesy of the writer John Osborne and the director Tony Richardson. For them he played Jimmy Porter in the film of *Look Back In Anger* and George Holyoake in the television drama *A Subject for Scandal and Concern*. He was marvellous in both parts and although there were to be several comments on his being rather too old for many people's concept of Jimmy Porter (when he made the film Burton was thirty-four whereas the play had been written by a playwright in his mid-twenties and the part created on the stage by Kenneth Haigh who had been precisely that age) it is not fanciful to speculate that given time a really fruitful relationship might have developed between Burton on the one hand and Osborne and his associates at the Royal Court on the other. It is only with the publication of his later autobiographical writings that we have been allowed to see the extent to which the young Osborne was fascinated by his own Welshness. His father came from Newport, as a youth the writer had been dubbed "a Welsh Fulham upstart", his first attempt at a play had concerned "a poetic Welsh loon", as an actor he had toured Wales and in *Look Back In Anger* for no apparent reason Jimmy Porter was given a Welsh foil in the character of Cliff. Within a month or so of his new fame Osborne was writing a part especially for Olivier and so perfect was Burton to be in the George Holyoake television play that it is not inconceivable that he would have written plays in which Welsh anger could have been more fully expressed.

Even more than with Jimmy Porter it was with the character of Bill Maitland in his 1964 play *Inadmissible Evidence* that Osborne let loose anger on the London stage and he was lucky enough to find the twenty-six year old Scottish actor Nicol Williamson to flesh out a part that was very much in Burton's range. But these were all might-have-beens for Burton had gone and whilst young talent contrived to flourish at the Royal Court the reinvigorated classical theatre became more and more concentrated in the hands of two men, Laurence Olivier and Peter Hall, and it was they who largely determined the new hierarchy of acting within the national culture. Olivier's respect for the man whom he clearly regarded as a peer was such that he often discussed with Burton the possibility of his joining the National Theatre. By the 1960s it was apparent that he could only return to London in that kind of superstar guise but it would have meant returning to a really quite alien world of politics and of management. In any case Olivier had in effect scooped the glory and Hall the power; they could never really be rivalled.

There were to be many theatre-goers who regretted that the age of Gielgud and Olivier had not evolved into one dominated by Scofield and Burton. In very different circumstances there might have been such a progression but the widely anticipated era of 'Sir Paul' and 'Sir Richard' was never to be. Perhaps neither actor had Olivier's range, his lightness, his comic touch, his love of disguise, costume, and the sheer challenge of transforming himself, let alone his political ambition and tenacity, but there can be no doubt that by the standards and expectations of English theatre in the mid- 1950s both Scofield and Burton had established themselves as the rightful heirs and had seemed to guarantee the relevance and legitimacy of classical theatre as it had been marketed since the 1930s. Certainly this pair were the last to assume the mantle of greatness within the framework of that actor-dominated theatre but as the theatre entered a period notable for its anger and kitchen-sink realism few could have realised that a new golden age for British acting was about to begin. For a few years the writers were the people in the news and then a largely director-controlled theatre was to emerge in which new works were blended with the standard repertoire but whatever the production there would be utterly professional and meticulous acting, the casting was always just right and every few seasons a new sensation would emerge and would become the player of the moment. Perhaps nobody quite had the stunning sexual impact of Burton and nothing quite was to rival the 'bobbysoxer idolatory' of his his Old Vic season but there was to be a steady line of greatness and there were to be fine Hamlets, Lears, and Coriolanuses offered by actors who would also turn up in the newest British and American plays. The New Wave of the 1950s had sent exciting messages throughout the nation and to London from all parts of the Empire came the likes of Albert Finney, Frank Finlay, Ian Richardson, Alan Howard, Derek Jacobi, Nicol Williamson, Anthony Hopkins, Michael Gambon, Ian McKellen and Antony Sher all of whom had the enormous advantages of being trained within a well established metropolitan theatre culture and of being sustained by the constraints and relative anonymity of ensemble acting. The capital now lionises its great actors in a slightly more dignified and restrained way in part because it rather takes them for granted.

Meanwhile Richard Burton was lost to the London stage and only returned to any kind of stage intermittently and very much within the kind of framework in which he had succeeded initially. In other words he was never to be an actor within a writers' or directors' theatre, he was never to be an ensemble player, he was never to be a part of a national redefinition of drama's role within the culture. A live performance by him was always offered as an event; he was a rather rootless personality who came on as a star attraction making what those awful television movies would describe as a 'special guest appearance'. Individual theatre-goers would fortuitously find that they had the opportunity to see him but the occasion would be unpredictable and largely meaningful only for itself. As far as Britain was concerned what was quite astonishingly to be his only appearance was in *Doctor Faustus* at the Oxford Playhouse. Here was a reminder that it was as a fine speaker of verse that he had first come into theatre but the performance rather divided the critics: his breathlessness and unfamiliarity with the text indicated that the discipline of the great stage actor had gone. Faustus apart his live roles were confined to North America and in particular to Broadway where he had first appeared in 1950 and where between 1960 and 1983 he was to achieve considerable success and widespread publicity in three roles with which for New Yorkers his name will always be associated. Of the three the first was probably the least demanding but it was also the most important both because it suggested his suitability for a part in the film of *Cleopatra* and because he exuded genuine star quality at a time when it was in short supply on Broadway. As a musical Lerner and Loewe's *Camelot* was never in the same class as their earlier *My Fair Lady* and considerable surgery was needed, not least from Philip Burton, before it emerged in an acceptable form but in the rôle of the king it offered the perfect vehicle for Richard Burton to establish his New York credentials. The whole affair, as Kenneth Tynan noted, was no more than "adult pantomime" but some kind of success was guaranteed if the king actually looked like a king and could convey genuine royal dilemmas. In New York audiences would be rather less inclined to wonder if the legs were those of a peasant rather than a king but would certainly appreciate that the head, torso, voice (both when singing and speaking) and the bearing were indeed majestic. It is difficult to imagine a character more perfect for Burton than that of Arthur: he had, as Tynan once again noticed, the "weight", the presence that suggested authority and commanded attention. There was ample freedom in the part for him to overcome his boredom by varying the text, the accent, and the mood and yet in essence he had to achieve a mix of charm and melancholy, the very qualities that had marked the playing of his earlier classical roles. It all came very easily.

There was to be considerable interest in his other two major Broadway roles but in both cases more serious questions were asked and the fascination of critics was now essentially with the darker side of his personality. In 1964 he starred in what became Broadway's longest-running *Hamlet*. In a production directed by the previous record-holder John Gielgud he gave one hundred and thrity-six consecutive performances and set a target that one suspects will never be surpassed. Appreciating his star's aversion to costume Gielgud had opted for a modern-dress version and so Burton came before his audiences dressed as if for rehearsal. The effect of the dark casual sweater was quite stunning: at first it seemed as if the man was a dancer or again a jazz musician, certainly the confrontation was going to be immediate and direct. There was a nakedness about him: nothing would be hidden in this production. Quite memorably Graham Jenkins was to say of his brother's performance that it was a case of watching "Richard Burton playing Richard Burton playing Hamlet". That neatly conveys some of the difficulty that the production had in sustaining a consistent interpretation and also the problems that the other players would have in relating to the Prince, but it also reminds us of the way in which a visit to the play was very much an exposure to a star personality who was powerfully revealing his innermost self. As the time approached for the pre-Broadway first night in Toronto press coverage and speculation had reached quite mammoth proportions and the critic David Cobb very nicely anticipated what was to occur in a headline that read 'Hamlet all set to star in Richard Burton'.

This *Hamlet* was being offered to a city that prided itself on its critical approach to theatre and in particular to acting techiques and nothing else that Burton was to do in his whole career was to be subjected to such minute analysis. There was only one question to be answered and that was whether this international superstar and personality about whom there had been so much gossip and rumours could turn on the power that had once made him one of the giants on the London stage. And the answer to that question was both yes and no. Yes, Burton was a formidable actor; to Walter Kerr he was "one of the most magnificently equipped actors living" possessing repose, intelligence, wit and a voice "that seems to prove that sound spirals outwards". Dwight MacDonald too found that the voice was "an extraordinary musical instrument" whilst Henry Hewes enjoyed its "sustained blasts of power and the sudden sharp staccato". Harold Clurman appreciated many of his "splendid personal attributes" but again it was the "power-ful" and "excellent" voice that mattered most; "its force might smash a windowpane". The actor was making his impact but the trouble was that none of these distinguished and formidable critics could see how all these outstanding personal qualities were in any way contributing to an understanding of Hamlet as a character. There was not much enthusiasm for the production and to an extent Gielgud was made to carry much of the blame with Dwight MacDonald in particular commenting on the ill-assort-ment of "at least four unharmonized acting styles" and on how much is missed in any *Hamlet* that fails to see it as essentially a story of court intrigue. For MacDonald as for the other critics the production was clearly a failure but eventually the director was less guilty than the star. Between them there seems to have been a general consensus that there was a coldness and lack of feeling in his playing and consequently that there was no real interpreta-tion of the Prince to which critics and scholars in the audience could respond. For MacDonald he was more a Mercutio than a Hamlet, more "a teddy boy than a prince", whilst Walter Kerr found that there was "a defeating coolness at the heart of the venture", it was an "automated fury" that was on display: there was a sound of hammering on stage but no splinters were flying up. Clurman found him somewhat distracted, not fully engaged and "as a result his agony and indignation often seemed little more than churlishness". "He appeared unhappy enough" he concluded, "but not about anything in the play".

We do not have to rely entirely on this absorbing critical debate for Burton's performance lives on in television film that was recorded in the theatre over two evenings. There are obvious dangers in generalising about his stage acting from what was a very primitive form of recording live drama especially as we now know about the way he relieved his boredom by nightly varying both his interpretation and his own physical preparedness for the part, but obviously it is impossible to ignore this priceless evidence. In many respects the film would seem to contradict the critical consensus. Certainly all the parts of the action do not cohere and there are long passages when the actor is clearly distracted and on auto-pilot but Burton is much more fully at ease with the rest of the company than any of the reviews suggested. There is real princely authority in all dealings with lesser folk and with the players, tenderness in the scenes with Gertrude and genuine warm humour between him and those who are obviously his friends. The physical presence is very different from that which one expects, the skin is bad, the frame small and far less robust than that suggested in the movies proper; it is a delicate body but its movements are those of a dancer. The voice at first is far from impressive; it is certainly a very Welsh voice, a posh Welsh voice in that Dylan Thomas vein so beloved by New Yorkers, but the lines are spoken so astonishingly quickly that many of the words are lost, some are garbled, some are barked, some are unnaturally and unaccountably shouted and occasionally there is a hoarseness and an angry choking. We are always hurried on to the soliloquies as if it is generally assumed that only they really matter and in fact when they arrive they are outstandingly brilliant and memorable. The enunciation is suddenly perfect with every word receiving the right emphasis and our attention is riveted but not only because of the voice; his very preoccupation commands our interest as does the prisoner-like starkness of his dress. Most surprisingly of all there is the total correctness of all his movements which drive home the point of the text every bit as much as his pronunciation and vocal emphasis. The man is more dapper and balletic than expected; this is a choreographed Hamlet of enormous delicacy in which naturally graceful movement and perfect timing are always sustaining the emotion required. He stamps out the phrase "quintessence of dust" as he climbs over the simple furniture, he visibly shrinks as he retreats into his natural coal-miner's crouch during the mad scenes, and in the "rogue and peasant slave" speech his every gesture bespeaks despair. There is acting here of the very highest quality and one aches with regret at not having been in the New York theatre.

It is quite fascinating to read those oh so precise and clever American reviews and then to see the filmed performance for oneself. One can fully appreciate many of the reservations and yet one feels that there was a rather petty and grudging reluctance to submit to the power that Burton injected into the crucial scenes in those early days before he grew bored with the enterprise. For some reason the acting or possibly just the approach irritated the critics into overstatement. One takes MacDonald's point that Burton had "no middle range" but then to claim that he failed to establish Hamlet as either a prince or an intellectual would appear to be wildly inaccurate. Similarly Clurman's so memorably amusing line that this was "not a bad Hamlet but rather no Hamlet at all" would seem merely gratuitous. The film would seem to suggest, to this observer at least, that New York was offered an intelligent and deeply felt interpretation of Hamlet in which the smack of real authority was combined with a very appropriate mix of warmth and despair. One can sense the problem though when a powerful actor offers more of himself than is strictly required in a formal presentation of the role. Perhaps this Dane has too much royal authority, too much intelligence and wit and more crucially too much despair and melancholy. The truth was, of course, that nobody could forget that this was Richard Burton. The reminders were irritatingly there when he rushed through the lesser speeches or slightly overdid the anger but even more they came in those moments when one realised that what was on display was his own distraction and his own sadness. Every critic is allowed to catalogue those moments that did not work but there was a suggestion with this production that their fastidious efforts to express their dissatisfaction were set in motion by their inability to cope with either the power or the melancholy of the man. He was just giving too much.

There was to be one final Broadway success and that was in the part of the psychoanalyst Martin Dysart in Peter Shaffer's play *Equus*. It had been twelve years since *Hamlet* and now every critic and indeed every theatre-goer knew almost everything there was to be known about Burton's health, private life and drinking. Here then was another guest performance in a part that had already been established by Anthony Hopkins and Anthony Perkins and which he was using essentially as a warm-up for the film version. The critics made their way to the theatre rather resentful of the way in which they were being used in having to comment on this sad and ageing superstar's antics. Once again they expected to see too much of the man in a play that would crumble under his presence. In fact they were to be overwhelmed both by his power and by his rightness in the part. Essentially they were giving thanks once more for the opportunity of seeing physical greatness in the theatre. For Walter Kerr this Dysart was the best work of Burton's life and all his "exclusively theatrical powers" were being used in a magnificent justification of live theatre. The voice "swept the walls of theatre clean with an apparently effortless power" and the audience was left "stunned and breathless"; the acting was restless, edgy, furious, passionate and intense; his physical presence was "radiating more than the sum of its own known energies, working on a scale greater than it is, pacing space on an arc more sweeping than is properly natural, more alive than 'live' ". Suddenly New York could appreciate great acting of a kind rather different from that which its coaches and critics had argued for twenty years earlier. Belatedly the scribes made their peace with a power and a presence that had never ceased to fascinate both London and Broadway audiences. Certainly here was an actor that had never been properly trained, that had never wanted to submit his talent to excessive directional discipline, and had broken all the rules by becoming quickly bored with the text.

Here too though was a star who thrilled and excited in a uniquely theatrical way. As Rod Steiger has often argued, true theatre-lovers always know that there is such a thing as great acting and that rare phenomenon depends in part on natural talent, instinct, charm and also to an extent on what the individual actor is prepared to put at risk. His own fear will communicate its own kind of tension and that tension will be doubled if the actor is giving something of himself away. Quite simply Richard Burton had presented to some very lucky theatre-goers a Prince Hal, a King Henry V, a Coriolanus, an Iago and a Hamlet as fine as any seen in modern times. Here indeed was Olivier's heir illuminating Shakespeare by the same kind of lightning as Garrick and Kean and yet unlike those great predecessors he was never an actor who could take refuge in the parts. What audiences saw on stage was the man himself putting his body, voice, intelligence and anxieties at the disposal of the part. It is no wonder that he was frightened away from that degree of painful self-exposure. For Burton the stage could never be that means of fulfilment or of a comfortable escape from personal uncertainty that it was for so many actors, for the very moment he created a part was the one in which he most fully saw through himself.

II
Barrymore's Heir

II
Barrymore's Heir

In his dismissal of Richard Burton as a film actor the critic David Thomson spoke of how the star had "never been able to shake off the image of a latter-day Barrymore". Born John Blythe in Philadelphia in 1882, the son of an English father and an American mother, John Barrymore developed as a leading stage actor to such an extent that in the early 1920s he gave both Broadway and London audiences what many thought to be the most fully satisfactory Hamlet ever. The claims for Barrymore's greatness, however, have not gone unchallenged and there have been many sceptics who have suspected that it was as much myth as memory that sustained the legend. We are back to the old "sculpting in snow" dilemma of assessing performances of the past but of course there is evidence for the anti-Barrymore school and that evidence is to be found on film. His film career was to last for almost thirty years and his much vaunted profile became as famous as any in the world, but in film after film his handsomeness does not disguise what David Thomson sums up as the "flamboyance", "ham" and "fraudulence" of his acting. Sensing his total unsuitability for the medium Barrymore appeared in the movies not as an actor but as a parody of one. Meanwhile he took the women Hollywood offered and spent his earnings on drink. Amidst his legacy of films there are those in which, in the words of Ethan Mordden "he is clearly sopping wet, staggering and mumbling". On Broadway Burton was, for some at least, clearly Barrymore's heir, but was he his successor too in the dreadfully ironic way in which the memory of those beautifully sculptured theatrical roles was to be eclipsed by whole archive shelves of filmed dross, ham and self-abuse? *The Everyman Companion to the Theatre* neatly sums up the common view of Burton's two acting careers by suggesting that he was "the twentieth-century theatre's leading sacrifice to the technological revolution". He was a formidable stage actor who opted for the movies and who opted for them in an almost uniquely exclusive way. In any study of his career the crucial question concerns what it was other than boredom that kept him away from theatre audiences hungry for his presence. First though, it is necessary to fill out his identity as an actor by attempting to establish precisely why it was that he was so indifferent in his chosen medium of the movies. Both socially and intellectually Theatre is an elitist art form whereas the movies have traditionally been seen as merely a popular pastime and for this reason, as the Everyman quote indicates, it has been almost impossible for Burton's career choice to be dismissed neutrally. For both London's and New York's theatreland he had fallen from grace, he had defected, he had opted for mindless entertainment and for personal wealth over the expectations of intellectuals; in short he had gone to Hollywood. His decision was patently a case of bad judgement and bad manners. It was also perhaps self-destructive for such was the jealousy of some playgoers that they thought of film as something which actively took away whatever distinction he had earlier possessed. First he cheapened himself and then, as with Barrymore, it began to show. Mordden is certainly of this school of thought and he boldly announced that Burton "ruined his talent in film work". Was it really quite that simple? There have been actors, as Mordden willingly admits, who whatever their preference for film and theatre, can achieve some kind of balance: Olivier, Richardson and Finney are the examples cited. Can film work actually destroy talent or is it rather than the film camera is utterly remorseless in highlighting physical imperfection and the ordinary even as it begins to strip away levels of disguised personality? Was it not really the case with Burton and with Barrymore that their lifestyles had led to a dependence on a branch of the entertainment business for which they had little respect and which paid them back by publicly chronicling the growth of an emptiness that their real-life charm and energy had somewhat obscured?

He had never come to terms with earning his living on the stage and so it is hardly surprising that Burton never took film seriously. He made fifty-five films and yet that academic discipline of film studies that has sprouted in recent years and which in part has been much concerned with the elements of acting has never deigned to praise him or indeed to give him any attention. In this respect he was surely collecting his just desserts for it is not easy to disagree with David Thomson's suggestion that he was probably a man "always a little contemptuous of the cinema". More recently Melvyn Bragg has both made and illustrated the point that it really is quite remarkable how little serious consideration he ever gave to the business or, rather we should say, the art of making movies. Even the most irresponsible tearaway actor thrown up by the American tradition of mumbling minimalist realism has shown more respect for the loyalty of audiences and for the earnestness of those scholars wanting to analyse 'their work' than did Burton. Although a man of the people, proud of his proletarian credentials and of his Socialist values, he was always to display the kind of indifference to the more serious claims of the movies that was characteristic of a feisty London drama critic or of an old-fashioned grammar-school teacher. As with the stage we are brought back to the way in which he took his own ability, beauty and charm for granted and confidently expected success and acclaim. Similarly the facility of early breakthrough never suggested that there was anything amiss: it was all a matter of collecting money for even older rope than he offered on the stage once the critics had departed. Even more regrettable was the fact that in the movies, to an extent that even surpassed his theatrical experience, there was nobody of sufficient genius and authority to tell him at that early stage that things could be different and better. Once again his physical qualities and, certainly inside the studios, his intellectual prowess as well were so taken for granted and were so unchallenged that there was no serious possibility of his being taken aside and informed of what his approach to film should have been. In the theatre he had by-passed some of the conventional training because at least he had been trained to speak verse and to project his voice but in front of the camera he had assumed, as presumably did many of those on the production side, that his mere presence would be enough and that there was nothing to be learned. Of course there were always producers and directors who knew what the movies were about but it was an industry that in part disguised its qualitative achievements inside a relentless hit-or-miss process in which many films and much talent was just written off. Trial and error was the way of the movies and if the camera found that something worked then it was 'bonanza' time. Perhaps it has only been with hindsight that scholars have been able to identify the elements that the camera demands and in terms of successful acting we realise that both a kind of photogenic beauty and a disciplined profession professionalism are required. Ultimately we may decide that Richard Burton failed in both respects but what was most crucial in determining the utter mediocrity of his film career was his failure to take the business seriously. He never devoted time to thinking about the true nature of the exercise and again it shows.

As with the theatre it was Emlyn Williams who provided the breakthrough and now almost half a century later we can see how that in itself was something of a false start for it meant that Burton really went into films from the wrong direction and at the wrong time. Williams was truly a theatrical type, a writer and an actor who instinctively knew what would work on the stage and who brought to the world of film the same kind of sheer professionalism. He was to prove to be a fairly natural screen villain but his technique and gestures were essentially melodramatic and earmarked him very much as a man of the repertory theatre and perhaps of the decade of the 1940s. His spendid dramatic writing is redolent of that context and although his 1948 film *The Last Days of Dolwyn* continues to please, its pleasures are really those which allow us insights into a world of fictional melodrama, Gothic overstatement and character stereotyping that were born in the age of Dickens and were just about running out of meaning in the decade after the Second World War. On film then as on stage, Richard Burton's debut comes at the end of a tradition rather than at a point of breakthrough or take-off. His first professional stage appearance in 1943 had been in Williams' *The Druid's Rest* and his role had essentially been that of the playwright as a boy, but he was already too old to appear in what was to prove the same author's most distinguished piece of autobiographical writing, for *The Corn is Green* had been written five years earlier when Burton was only thirteen and still undiscovered. In 1945 he did the play on radio but he was too late for the movie from Warner Bros, a studio that loved Victorian melodrama of the rags to riches kind, and who filmed the play that year as a vehicle for Bette Davis and with John Dall as the young miner who makes it to Oxford. And yet Burton was clearly born to play the part of Morgan Evans, it was quite simply his own story. Emlyn Williams had sensed that his young *alter ego* had now arrived and yet quite tantalisingly the moment for this to be exploited had gone. There was always to be this frustration of Burton being culturally just out of 'sync'. It was a career disoriented, like so many others, by National Service and after completing his first film with Williams in 1948 he found himself as a twenty-four year old looking for new and different ways in which a relatively young cinematic talent could be expressed. It can be argued that he had to wait a decade before he was given his first successful opportunity.

Between *The Last Days of Dolwyn* which was made in 1948 and the *Look Back in Anger* of 1959 Burton made twelve films and in so doing passed from youth into what was almost middle age, and from being a promising newcomer into a star personality. He first made four films for those British studios which at that time were rather hopelessly trying to establish some kind of identity and to hang on to some kind of market in the face of an American dominance that had once again been rather painfully underlined following the 1947 economic crisis. In part the trouble really was financial: American films were superbly made and the smaller British industry, which could only ever hope to get a tiny number of its prestige films into the lucrative American market, was forced to make a large number of routine support films to fill out programmes and quota requirements. This wholly subservient role within the English-speaking world of films had merely helped to perpetuate a pattern in which the British studios failed to attract either original writing of any merit or technical personnel who thought of themselves as being cinematic innovators or creators. What limited talent did develop at the behest of British producers was channelled into prestige productions in which workmanlike and very professional directors would use adapted material within restricted genres which confirmed American myths about Britishness just as it left unchallenged the traditional social range and melodrama of indigenous middle-brow fiction. The greater part of the British film industry was merely going through the motions; of course it could respond to fashions being set either in Hollywood or elsewhere in the culture but only in a way that was several steps removed from any really innovative talent.

And so it was that Burton's third film *Waterfront* saw him cast as an unemployed Liverpool ship's engineer in an adaptation of a novel by John Brophy directed by Michael Anderson. This was the period some five years after the war and at the height of the Cold War when producers both in Hollywood and London had realised that the steady diet of war films and mindless romance had to be augmented by just a whiff of social realism and when discreetly the tensions associated with labour, with race and with youth were just beginning to permeate into supporting features. Of course Italian Neo-Realism had spectacularly pointed the way but if the English-language films wanted to compete in those intellectually pleasing stakes then some kind of genuinely pion- eering writing, directing and acting commitment was needed. For years the critics in London and New York had been baying for a breakthrough into social and emotional realism and yet the pro- ducers continued to tease by offering routine films like *Waterfront* which all but escaped serious critical notice. Certainly the time was ripe for a film dealing with unemployment in a major port but Burton's tragedy was that he had wandered onto the water- front just a little too early. The Americans were to get there in a vastly more challenging way just four years later courtesy of the talents of Budd Schulberg, Elia Kazan and Marlon Brando. As always it took the British a little longer to achieve breakthrough but the absolute inevitability of that should not prevent us from speculating on what could have been. Liverpool was about to explode in cultural terms and surely, if the dates were just a little different, a Lindsay Anderson, who was to be fascinated by *On the Waterfront* and who had directed his first documentary in 1940, could have met up with the North Wales born Liverpudlian playwright Alun Owen who was to give Scouse its first poetic and dramatic form in the 1950s and with him created a waterfront role for Burton which would have been more of a hand-grenade within the culture than the mere competence offered in Michael Ander- son's rather drab film.

At Stratford, in his four British films, and to an extent on Broadway, Burton had proved two things to Hollywood's satisfaction. He had shown that he had 'class', and what was more important as far as they were concerned, that he had enough intelligence to be able to follow a simple command. And so Hollywood bought him just as it had every other bit of walking, talking and writing talent for the last few decades. He was simply one more investment that might or might not pay off. As it happens his transfer was carried out between the presiding geniuses of the two respective national cinemas for Alexander Korda lent him to Darryl F. Zanuck. However, being in the hands of entrepreneurial and artistic greatness was no guarantee of acting success, the right vehicle always had to be to hand. In the studios there always had to be a coming together of an actor, a role and a director's seeing eye. Burton had been borrowed by Zanuck in the expectation that something would turn up but at the outset there would have been no great illusions. Olivier had been bought as a hot property but in the end had only been moderately successful as a screen charmer, his appearance confirming what Barrymore had already suggested, that the studios had 'more demanding' standards than Shakespeare. It was very much as a potential Olivier that Burton had been picked up, as was the case with James Mason who was taken from the British studios at very much the same time and as part of the same exercise by which it was hoped to keep going a tradition of what was thought of as totally respectable and utterly well-bred and well-spoken English sexual charm. Both Mason and Burton were unlucky in their timing although it must be admitted that the former brought the tradition to an end very honourably. Masculinity in American films had always been a matter of fashion and Cold War America was now in the process of identifying a new range of indigenous heroes and anti-heroes. Much of what was best in American movies and certainly much of the best acting was to come either in the already established genres or in allegorical drama in which new political and sexual tensions were explored. Across the board there was an enormous deepening both of the psychological and social sophistication of the American film and not surprisingly in what was to be the decade of Brando, Dean and Clift there was less prestigious writing for the traditional English romantic type. Meanwhile the outstandingly gifted Cary Grant was always there to provide Mid-Atlantic charm, class, sexual danger and especially deft comedy. Outside the genres and the new American drama it was bound to be a difficult time for a British romantic with classical qualifications and clearly in his Hollywood films of the 1950s Burton is a man for whom a niche had not been found.

He was off to a good start for he received an Academy nomination for his role in *My Cousin Rachel* but here he had been lucky in a way that he was rarely to be in subsequent years for he was just right for this Olivier-type role in what was a Victorian melodrama. Thereafter he came on to the screen as the Roman centurion in a religious epic, as an English officer in the North African army, as Edwin Booth the great American Shakespearean actor of the last century, as a Hindu doctor and as the emperor Alexander the Great. None of this was the stuff of cinematic greatness or of cultural relevance. Hollywood operated on so many levels and these were for the most part big roles in which much was invested but they were all films aimed at the suburbs and at the respectable lower middle-class and upper working-class married couples who were thought of as the ballast of film audiences. But with so much precise work going on in the genres and with the expectations of the young and the rebellious being aroused by new styles of writing and directing it was perhaps inevitable that Burton would find himself rather adrift in films blandly fashioned for these complacent suburbs. A longer run in costume melodrama might have allowed him to find his feet and the Fox executives to do a little more thinking. Once again he had made his debut in a film that came at the end of a tradition and thereafter he was at the beck and call of a studio that was looking for a return on its investment without giving much thought to his needs and which was setting up each film in ways that varied from the slap-dash to the crass. He was at least competent as the soldier in *The Desert Rats*, but elsewhere the inadequate and even stupid thinking that had assembled the films never allowed him to give any real meaning to his roles. Perhaps he was born to play Roman centurions and Greek scholar-soldiers but not in a cloyingly emotional, tasteless and rather morbid tale dominated by the Crucifixion on the one hand or in a very dull epic in which he had to wear a ridiculous wig on the other. Given his talent, his looks and the money available, these were opportunities that should not have been missed.

That was especially the case with *The Prince of Players* where surely better directing might have resulted in one of the finest Shakespearean films ever. It is wonderful to have these fine glimpses of Burton the young classical actor but it was so evident that very little thought had been given to the quality of the script, to how the Shakespearean set-pieces could be integrated into the story or to how Burton could have adapted his own theatrical style to the film studio or to conveying the more declamatory style of his legendary predecessor. With all these films we can see how Hollywood had lost its touch. The vast sums of money involved and the emphasis on the epic, exotic and melodramatic were sure signs of panic in the face of the challenge of television, whilst the restless search for safe middle-brow themes and settings testified to Hollywood's inability to gauge the real mood and need of the newly affluent public with its more carefully hidden anxieties.

Burton had been hired to take class and romance into the suburbs and that is what he had proceeded to do but only in roles that attracted audiences who were there out of either habit or curiosity. In no sense was he a sensation and the public coolness was accompanied and sustained by critical disappointment and studio resignation. He was not going to be a cult figure and perhaps not even a versatile studio man who could be permanently kept in work in obvious parts. Zanuck had felt forced to acquire him just because he was the new Olivier and to prevent the other companies from getting him, but in truth his expectations had not been high as he thought him rather "too fat" for a romantic lead. In cinematic terms the newcomer had just not fitted in and one can sense this from a simple perusal of the fan magazines and press hand-outs, for Burton's features were not quite young and innocent enough for adolescent readers nor yet craggy and world-weary enough to appeal just in terms of personality; it was not an American face but neither was it Irish or Italian or Jewish although there were some bizarre attempts by make-up to bring out the exotic. Overall by the very singular standards of the publicity still and of the screen, the face was too full and round and the head too square: certainly he was not fat but in Hollywood it was the proportions that were all important and the fact was that he was too broad given his height. All in all it had not been a successful collaboration, the parts were not right, too much had been taken for granted and gradually the suspicions were confirmed that he was not a natural screen actor, or at least he did not have that lightness and that controlled animation that the camera was always confirming as the essence of cinematic style. For his supporters in London all this came really as confirmation of Hollywood's inferiority and lack of judgement but we should pause to recall how effortlessly talent was being used effectively in other parts of the factory production line. Brando blazed on to the screen as the paraplegic in *The Men* and then went on in those early years of the fifties to create some of the most memorable rôles in film history. Critics throughout the world were thrilled by his acting in *A Streetcar Named Desire, The Wild Ones* and *On the Waterfront* and not a few of them were intrigued by his Mark Antony in Shakespeare's *Julius Caesar*. Similarly James Dean had not waited long before he spotted the potential of *East of Eden* and Montgomery Clift had made *Red River* within a year of being discovered. Hollywood was a sophisticated and an excited place but sadly Burton was missing the vital action. He had been culturally and physically misunderstood and wrongly identified. It was not entirely his fault that he had wandered into a world that was alien to him at a time when it was redefining its own notions of adolescence and of sexuality but certainly he must be blamed for not ensuring that his talent was available for use precisely at the point within his own culture that he thought most exciting and relevant. All actors need luck but great actors need a felicity of judgement too.

It was only in 1959 that Burton made a film in which he could meaningfully draw on his own beliefs, passions and values. As we have seen it was courtesy of John Osborne, Tony Richardson and *Look Back in Anger* that he was able to squeeze in a contribution to the artistic and cultural transformation that was going on in his own country. So rarely was he to touch the pulse of his native culture that one shudders with horror at the thought that he might have missed making this film. It was seen by only the smallest fraction of the audience that had been attracted by the epic qualities of *The Robe* and in general neither the film nor his performance was much liked by the critics. For many it was a dull, drab, unpleasant story in which a very theatrical actor who was too old for the part seemed continuously out of sorts for reasons which they could work up no sympathy. For Campbell Dixon the hero Jimmy Porter was just "schizoid or a paranoic", whilst for Bosley Crowther the film presented "the emotional vandalism" of "a conventional weakling and crybaby". For John Russell Taylor, Burton was too substantial~ too well-fed for a character who needed to be depicted as "a weedy neurotic" whilst for Alexander Walker this Jimmy Porter lacked the "class-conscious sharpness" required and which called for an actor who was far more obviously from a proletarian background. Three years earlier when his play was first performed, John Osborne must have taken the anger of most critics as the first evidence that he had touched a few nerves within the culture, and similarly the mere fact that there was critical debate and anger over Tony Richardson's film indicated that at least intelligent observers were beginning to care about things within the previously bland world of British films. Critical discomfort and embarrassment were a sure sign of changing standards and debate and discussion indicated a new pattern of expectation. Osborne had created a buzz within circles that mattered and now that buzz returned as one of the country's most famous actors offered a new version of Jimmy Porter even if the populace as a whole could not have cared less. This screen rôle of Burton's is part of our cultural history, it is important evidence in any understanding of what the 1950s meant as a decade.

Both Pauline Kael and Alexander Walker were amongst the admirers of Osborne's play who saw Jimmy Porter as a modern Hamlet who soliloquises about how things are not all well in the state of England and his own difficulty in alighting on action that could put things right. In America Brando and Dean had been needed to express the confusion of the time but in Britain it was not at all inappropriate that the latent energy and protest that was accumulating in pubs, coffee bars, jazz clubs, student unions and staffrooms should be expressed by an actor with the right feel for language and rhetoric and with the right degree of educational, provincial and sexual confidence. A confused and whingeing wimp might have been in keeping with some critical expectations but as Jimmy Porter, Burton's smack of authority was sure testimony of unused intellectual cultural and sexual energy. His tone and his anger was cutting through the formality and politeness

51

that passed for natural discourse in the 1950s. It was a nonsense to assume that such directness and power could be confined to the Old Vic or the Royal Court. The culture needed to be complicated and now was the moment for writers, intellectuals, artists and actors to open up every medium and vehicle that was to hand. Burton's own Jimmy Porter represented precisely and legitimately the challenge that British society now had to confront.

Alexander Walker and other historians have explained to what extent that flowering of the British cinema that occurred in the early 1960s was largely dependent on what proved to be a short-term coming together of North American investment and British managerial and creative energies. Osborne and Richardson had formed their own production company, Woodfall, but their film would never have got off the ground if it had not been for the deal the Canadian born producer Harry Saltzman had worked out with Warner who not only financed the film but accepted it as part of the actor's three-film obligation to them as a studio. What was by far Burton's most satisfactory and challenging film had come about through a conjunction of the most creative talents in London theatre on the one hand and English-language film production on the other and obviously this was the moment when Burton, whose reputation was vital for the whole success of the venture, should have more fully realised the direction in which his career should proceed. It was the richest context in which he had ever worked and it was the kind of arrangement he should have done everything to perpetuate. There were some savage reviews but there was sufficient praise from all those who really counted including Osborne himself to have brought him fully to his senses. We can see now that he should have done far more to make things happen and we can see too that this was the moment when a far more permanent cooperation between London's talent and New York's money should have been established. Saltzman and other producers were to set up some wonderful films in the next decade using the talents of Tom Courtenay, Albert Finney, Peter O'Toole, Nicol Williamson and above all Michael Caine and Sean Connery, but given Burton's American fame and contacts a full commitment to production by him might have allowed an even more rewarding mix of blockbuster and art movies.

Quite rightly Bragg has stressed how good Burton looks in *Look Back in Anger*. By 1959 his puppy fat and what Binkie Beaumont called "the fat and round face of a ploughboy" had gone; instead there was "the mature, virile, wonderfully and intelligently handsome man" of Bragg's description. There is also, of course, for those who viewed his films chronologically the shock of seeing him out of make-up and playing a thoroughly contemporary version of himself. His theatrical reputation and what were by London and Hollywood standards unconventional good looks and physique had suggested his suitability for epic, exotic and romantic roles but here was powerful and corrosive proof of his ability to make an impact in the new drama of his own national culture. We have already speculated about what could have been a very fruitful theatrical partnership with John Osborne, and given Burton's newly-acquired international status it would be far less fanciful to imagine a situation in which, working with directors like Richardson, Lindsay Anderson and Jack Gold and with other writers like Simon Grey, John Braine and Keith Waterhouse, he might have helped extend that cinematic breakthrough into contemporary realism that had occurred at the end of the fifties for just a little longer throughout the sixties. But that was not to be.

He went back to Hollywood and to more suburban melodrama until he once again donned Roman tunic to play Mark Antony in *Cleopatra*, his eighteenth film and the one that was to transform his life by more or less ensuring that he could never again be the leading man at the Old Vic or the central figure in a renaissance of British cinema. There were thirty-seven films to come over the twenty years or so of his life that remained and in some of them he was good, or at least effective, but poor films and totally unsuitable rôles predominate. More depressing though than the mediocrity of most of the films is the way that his choice of work prevented him from ever again being an actor operating at the cutting edge of either British or American contemporary cultural statements. In movies even more than with his live performances, he was a grandstanding guest personality more than a professional blending effortlessly and naturally into a part. His personality status continued with his limited and very predictable range to ensure disappointment and failure on two counts. He could never extend himself so as to create a character existing independently of his own persona and yet there was, with perhaps one notable exception, never an opportunity to play another role like that of Jimmy Porter in which he could feed quite naturally and intelligently off his own energies and his own social and intellectual identity. In film terms he was to become something of a grotesque and that embarrassment which many people experience when watching him on screen was only in part related to the badness of the film. A more contributory cause is the unpleasantness and surprise of seeing someone with whom one is so very familiar having nowhere to hide in the story in which he was appearing. He is unconvincing and disturbing because he is always Richard Burton. More than any other major star he was unable to submit himself to the basic rules of the medium. He never allows the magic of film to take over. Hence he hated to see himself on screen, he urged friends not to see his movies, and many of those who admire him find it only too easy to respect his wishes in this respect. The conventions of film make him, even in his better rôles, almost unwatchable.

Everyone will have their own particular nightmares about specific Burton roles. When he awoke with guilt in the middle of the night it was always *The Klansman* that he worried about most for he and Lee Marvin had been drunk throughout the whole shooting of the film and he had almost no memory of ever having made it. Vincent Canby had suspected something was wrong and had thought he was acting with "partial paralysis of the mouth". It was in *Candy* that he most fully exposed both how awfully boorish he could be when drunk and how limited were his comic talents. This was shown at greater length in *The Taming of the Shrew* where his attempt at jest becomes merely violent and in the homosexual film *Staircase* where his campness was heavy and distasteful. In this latter film there is a bath scene which reveals a thickening of the body and the onset of a drinker's pot and the still of that moment should be compared with the studio shot of him on the West Indian beach taken twelve years earlier. It was at this stage too that the face begins to become annoying. Rex Reed described it as "a gibbon's bottom" and Vincent Canby thought it potato-like, a comparison that reoccurred to him with a later film *Villain* where the face struck him as being "fat and soft like a potato". *Time Magazine* now spoke of his "piggy eyes".

In a sense the work of which he should have been most proud was the film version of the *Doctor Faustus* he had done in Oxford, for he financed, co-produced and co-directed the whole venture. Yet it was perhaps his most spectacular and bizarre failure. This was a labour of love and one which a great speaker of verse could legitimately have planned as a permanent record of his talent and yet to the leading American critic Pauline Kael his own reading of the role was "dead and muffled" and the movie in general was just "porny comic strip". Over and over again it is worthwhile to compare one's own embarrassment with these films with the recorded critical response in which the twin themes are first Burton's total lack of judgement and then a growing preoccupation with just how physically unsuited he was to many of the parts in which he appeared. There were clearly some rôles in which he no longer fulfilled the basic requirements of a movie star and yet running through many of the other films there are some satisfactory moments which occur in a pattern that points very definitely to what might have been. Several themes stand out.

He was often a soldier and there were occasions when he fulfilled that responsibility professionally and efficiently. Bragg has commented on his directness, "his lack of bullshit", when playing men of action. He looked good in uniform and he obviously enjoyed wearing it if only because it solved some of his worries about costume. Above all though there was the voice about which there was always something of the military. The young Welsh schoolboy trained by Philip Burton had obviously needed a model to work from and the ATC offered a context in which order and information were transmitted in a loud, clear and no-nonsense manner. Later there were the three years in the RAF to confirm the influence. He was as a type very much a trained serviceman of 1940s vintage and that always showed. Only very narrowly had he missed serving in the Second World War but in terms of his career what was more relevant was the way in which he was to miss out on that spate of British war films. Surely this was a genre in which he could have played some memorable rôles and it is especially regrettable that film never allowed him to join dufflecoated colleagues like Jack Hawkins, John Mills, Dirk Bogarde and John Grigson on the bridge of His Majesty's naval vessels. He was a born commander, one whose playing suggested coolness in the face of crisis, even a welcoming of it, and all the time the voice would snap or bark out impatient yet authoritative commands which seemed to promise victory or at least some enjoyment of the struggle. And yet this talent was never intelligently deployed in an action film. When in uniform he either gave the impression of a great actor being terribly underused or he just descended to the general level of mediocrity. Once again bad luck and bad judgement were to keep him away from the kind of script and film in which he could have made a real impact depicting some of the challenges and dilemmas of military command and the contrast here is with those actors like Alec Guinness, Jack Hawkins, James Mason, John Mills and George C. Scott who were to achieve greatness courtesy of Second World War heroes. He should have been asked to do much more whilst wearing a contemporary uniform but the greater loss was his failure to put on film Shakespeare's soldiers, some of whom he had earlier rendered quite brilliantly on stage. Films of Burton as Henry V and Coriolanus and also as a Mark Antony speaking Shakespeare rather than Mankiewicz would have given many people much satisfaction.

Frequently he was to appear as a priest and quite obviously producers and directors tended to think of him as soon as they had to cast a character who at some time or other had been in touch with God. He had first carried 'his cathedral' on to the stage in London and he was to be lumbered with it throughout nearly the whole length of his movie career. His 'conversion' had been a very public one for millions of people had seen *The Robe* and whatever the rumours about his own private life and the loss of faith he was meant to depict in certain of his priestly rôles it often seemed as if he was a man who had never really recovered from that early experience. He was an actor who had been picked up by Hollywood because it was hoped that he would convey on the screen the sexuality he exuded on the stage and in private and yet in the films that was only a part of what came across. He undoubtedly possessed animal qualities and the suggestion was that any kind of abstinence was quite beyond him. There could never by any question of him playing a puritan or the kind of saint that Henry Fonda could do so well and yet he seemed perfect for the man struggling to control his sexuality and his appetites precisely because he had been intellectually and spiritually in touch with some kind of divine authority if only in the distant past. In fact this was very definitely a question of intelligence for his powers of thought were evident especially when in repose and that always gave him a detachment that was unusual in a movies and which seemed to have its source in some kind of understanding. What elevated that intellectual dimension into a spiritual one, however, was an added sense of melancholy, of a man who was troubled possibly by his guilt, certainly by a loss of innocence, and one who was capable of fierce anger over the shabbiness of the world's compromises. His was a lived-in face and surely those eyes had seen something which had not allowed untroubled sleep.

Even more there was the voice for it was quite naturally that of a preacher and a believer. It was quite obviously a pulpit voice, one that demanded a cathedral and a congregation wanting full value and meaning and it was also a voice of instruction and of guidance; there was real authority in its didactic tone and its firm confidence would immediately reassure kneeling supplicants. With him we are often reminded of how closely the qualities of a good ruler or soldier approximate those of a religious counsellor. There was even more to the voice than this for the religious rhetoric of which it was capable was not just biblical and sermon-like, it also very easily slipped into incantation and into a ritual to which we the congregation might not always have easy access. The chant and other aspects of religious 'business' came to him so naturally that he always seemed to be in touch with and energised by some force that set him apart. What exactly that force might be though was a very moot point. It could be the Christian God that he encountered early on in *The Robe* and in *Beckett* but other directors were to feel that he was troubled by stranger forces and powers and his journey which had begun at the cross in the earlier of those films was to lead him much later to *The Exorcist II*. In general his troubled spiritual qualities were to be exploited rather than used intelligently. There were to be one or two films in which his religious melancholy was allowed some scope by good writing and directing but at this stage it must be once again regretted that a deeply explored crisis of faith never served as the basis of one of his films. His contemporary Paul Scofield was to be luckier.

A final possibility was suggested by the way in which he was used to play famous people or some of the great names in history.

He had effortlessly suggested royal and patrician status in the theatre and soon he became accepted in his own right as somebody who was internationally important and all of this made him very much in demand when any producer or director was casting a film about a great man. Again what was to be vital was the quality of the writing for otherwise his playing would once more look like exploitative grandstanding. Rod Steiger has spoken of how players like himself and Burton have a power and a presence and a bravery that producers always interpret in terms of that hateful phrase 'larger than life qualities' and it is precisely that which they hope will carry their prestige bio-pics. In the absence of a good script however the project can either fall flat or have to rely on good old-fashioned hamming. And so it was that Burton was what Bosley Crowther thought a very realistic Archbishop in what was for the most part a very dull *Beckett*. He was, as suggested by Vincent Canby, intelligent but "loutish" as Henry VIII in an equally dull *Anne of a Thousand Days* that was unfortunately based on a play by Maxwell Anderson rather than one by Shakespeare or Robert Bolt. Later Canby thought he made an excellent Trotsky for director Joseph Losey but again the majority of critics found themselves returning to the dominant quality of dullness. In Yugoslavia Burton went into action as the war-time Marshall Tito and there was some public celebration of how much a look-alike he was. Then at the end of his career he came on to the screen as a magnificently believable Wagner and as such had the pleasure of upstaging Sir Larry, Sir Ralph and Sir John but only in a rambling and not too carefully-made television spectacular. Finally he was determined to make a mark as someone who had almost become a real person within the culture and that was O'Brien the representative of Big Brother in a version of Orwell's *Nineteen Eighty-Four*. In all these rôles we can see what the producers were after and we can see also Burton himself striving to bring History alive as he attempts to act himself into it as an agent of something both powerful and significant. At times he was working from challenging scripts based on writing by authors such as Anouilh and Orwell, and with Losey at least he was working with a great director but none of these films survive as a masterpiece or even as an important contribution to the problems suggested by the reality of the careers of the characters themselves. Manifestly and tantalisingly he hints at the power and attraction that all those people would probably have had and yet neither the script nor his own reserve will quite allow that quickness of action and sharpness of response that converts potential into real history, a tableau into real art.

In any approach to Burton's film career it is easy to dwell on these themes of inappropriate casting and lost opportunity but mercifully there were a handful of films in which he has left memorable moments and in which his own personal qualities added to the meaning and impact of the whole. We have seen how within his own British culture he failed to establish a meaningful relationship with an indigenous writing talent and that this ensured his being cut off from the exciting development occurring even at the time he was committing himself to mediocre projects. Meanwhile in the United States, Tennessee Williams had transformed contemporary classics by using his own experiences to create plays in which actors were invited to reveal new layers of feeling as they tore away the hypocrisy of social and sexual conventions. The impact came first on the stage and then in a slightly sanitised and Bowdlerised version on the screen. New acting talent was needed for these works and, as we have seen, Brando was among the first to seize the opportunity. In 1964 Burton was given his chance when John Huston cast him as the defrocked priest Shannon in Wiilliams' *The Night of the Iguana*. The playwright himself disliked the film and Maurice Yacowar has explained how the film with its exotic Mexican settings and star-studded female cast, including the exuberant and beautiful Ava Gardner, rather avoided the sheer claustrophobia and hopelessness of the original play. Even with this more upbeat approach, however, the story remained too gloomy, too obscure and too wordy for most audiences. Williams' writing was always an acquired minority taste and the critic who lacked sympathy was always to see tedious melodrama. Bosley Crowther hated Huston's film: "who are these dislocated wanderers", he asked, and "why are they so aggressive in punching their loneliness home to the world?" He was particularly infuriated by Burton's acting which he blamed for ruining the whole venture: he found him "spectacularly gross, a figure of wild disarrangement", "farcical when he is not grotesque" and throughout "as curiously wild-eyed and ghostly as only Richard Burton can be". Here we have a classic summation of what often was thought by critics about most of his other roles but in this instance Crowther surely missed the extent to which the film benefited from the appropriate casting of Burton. So fully did the actor's whole appearance suggest a fall from grace and a surrender to the sins of the flesh that, as Yacowar has explained, many explicit scenes and references could conveniently be left out of the script. More than in any other film he ever made, Burton's mere presence was contributing significantly to the impact of the text and the action and he was additionally able to draw on so much of himself whether in guiding or preaching to his party of women students, exchanging ideas with Deborah Kerr, comically fumbling for sex with the nymphette Sue Lyon, or sparring with and gaining strength from the very sure acting of Ava Gardner. In part he was playing himself but more to the point was the way in which he was able to respond to the poetry of the writing and the nuances created by highly professional directing and ensemble acting. Here he was working in a totally intelligent and integrated context and the result was an extension of his range and a better balance between his positive and melancholic aspects.

He made only one other Tennessee Williams film and that was a version of the play *The Milk Train Doesn't Stop Here Anymore* that Joseph Losey brought to the screen as *Boom*. Nothing else that Burton did was to receive quite as much negative comment as this film and many critics have seen it as bringing together many of the worst aspects of the 1960s, the half-thought-out ideas of Williams, the pretentious art-house direction of Losey and the sheer exploitation of the Burton-Elizabeth Taylor relationship, without any careful reference to the dramatist's original intentions. Throughout the film there is a jarring between the magnificence of the Mediterranean cliff-top setting and Miss Taylor's thoroughly common version of Bankheadian flamboyance. She has never been so spectacularly miscast, so easy to hate, and that voice is shrill and squawkish enough to loosen the plasterwork. Alongside her Burton is quite magnificent. He appears on the island as a down-and-out romantic poet and soon is transformed courtesy of a samurai bath-robe into a veritable Greek king bestriding his palace. He is astonishingly handsome and he can be seen to be acquiring sheen, class and beauty in response to the Mediterranean sun. But above all he is a poet and clearly one whose voice and images have softened many a female heart just as unreliability would have lost him many friends. The original intention was to call the movie 'Goforth' after the Taylor character but the title was changed to *Boom* not least because of the way in which Burton so beautifully timed and modulated his first response to the sound of the waves breaking at the cliff bottom. His initial 'boom' brilliantly catches what the script wants to celebrate as "the shock of each moment of still being alive" and instantly convinces us that this indeed is a poet who has savoured life just as he anticipates death. Burton as Flanders quite naturally allows his very English poet to emerge as indeed the Angel of Death and with that one 'boom' allows all of us who have to rely now on his filmed work to experience the very genius of his acting and the power of his presence.

We can relish that moment in *Boom* even as we regret that he was not allowed other rôles in which he could suggest the poetic, act with such assumed irony and harness his own naturalism to the cause of allegory. For the most part the times were calling for a brasher realism and even with Tennessee Williams it was the social rather than the personal truth to which audiences responded. All the best parts were going to actors who could bring a proletarian or at least a classless edge to characters as they distanced themselves from the dated style and caste-shibboleths of ruling élites. It was in such a role that Burton would have to make his impact on a new generation of cinema-goers and obviously the move in this direction would represent a major challenge to an actor who was utterly proud of his protelarian background and rebellious nature and yet who always suggested himself to producers as a patrician and a man of grand rather than under-rated gestures.

In 1965 though the radical American director Martin Ritt invited him to play the hard-done-by British agent Leamas in a film of John le Carré's *The Spy Who Came in from the Cold* and in doing so he enabled Burton to create the rôle which most critics would adjudge his greatest on film. Manny Farber has written brilliantly about the way in which Ritt, aiming for a fully documentary effect, squeezed out of the action many of Leamas' moments of physical and spiritual strength because what he wanted from Burton was a man totally and hopelessly defeated, an utter cipher at the mercy of stronger forces. Bragg has explained too how throughout the making of the film Ritt was able to exploit the actor's quite considerable off-the-set drinking and sexual problems; maybe Burton was being 'used' every bit as much as the character he was portraying. In truth his playing in this film is very mixed and suggests the extent to which he was not fully in control. He actually looks at his most haunted in the initial interview in which he is asked to go 'back into the cold' whilst in later external shots in 'East Germany' he is remarkably handsome and dignified. He is appallingly hammy in scenes in which Leamas must feign drunkenness and anger and when he comes to the climax of the big speech about how espionage exploits its agents and must remain amoral he delivers it magnificently but as if to an Old Vic audience rather than to the girl he loves who is the sole passenger in his car. It is largely when in repose that Burton made his effective and unwitting contribution. Farber spoke of moments of surprising truthfulness and of a "powerful projection of something rocklike and stubborn in Leamas' character as to be good in its own right", whilst David Shipman saw an actor drawing on his "best qualities of misanthropy, determination and sardonic humour". It is hardly surprising though that the actor was not to do much more work in this vein, for not only was the director using him against type he was forcing him to relinquish the rhetoric and authority that were the central features of his armoury even as he was accentuating all the dark and negative aspects of his personality. Ritt was holding a mirror up to Burton's nature in a way that no other director was ever to do and was intimating to him that his future as an actor may lie in exploring both his own unattractiveness and his own emptiness. The critics all enthused about the realism of the movie, about its exposure of the cruel and very dull detail of the drudge-like way in which espionage was necessarily organised and about the relentless avoidance of glamour and sentiment but as they did this they were always brought back to how the truth of the *mise-en-scène* was sustained by the truth that the camera had found in Richard Burton. Kenneth Tynan reported on how, as the film progressed, his "dour and expressively ravaged face comes to resemble a bullet-chipped wall against which many executions have taken place". What the face was expressing above all else was the state of the soul that lay within.

A valuable lesson had been learned. Within some films there would be action, rhetoric or costume to encourage the positive and attractive aspects of Burton's personality but to work with those writers and directors who were exploring the anti-heroic would be to risk laying bare the dark side of his own nature. He was now far too vulnerable and wounded a person to take that risk and he was never again to let himself be stripped in quite that way with the result that another possible direction in which his talent could have gone was closed down. In only one other film did he work with another writer who was aware of the hollowness that lay behind the contemporary political rhetoric and the way in which the normal conventions of civilised society rested on specific cultural conditions. That writer was Graham Greene and the film was *The Comedians,* which dealt with a range of Western types who come together in an Haitian hotel. Critics were becoming more and more fascinated with that coming together of geographical back-waters and human despair that constituted 'Greeneland' but they were universally of the opinion that this was a pretty tired and two-dimensional attempt to create that world. The leading characters Jones, Brown and Smith were quite deliberately depicted as very ordinary commonplace whites who have wandered into a nightmare world of black politics but what is interesting is the extent to which Burton does so well in conveying what Bosley Crowther called the "acerbity and bristling boredom that seemed so natural in those circumstances". Here is a man who obviously has had the capacity for romance, action and heroics but now on Haiti has become aware of the utter futility of things. Inevitably he too becomes a bore, for Crowther "a fellow we've all endured many times". Again Burton had come to the service of contemporary fiction by revealing just how much of himself had normally been disguised by more positive theatrical and social questions. There was much of Mr Brown in Mr Burton.

Leamas was undoubtedly to be his most acclaimed rôle but in two other films he produced performances which will live on in popular memory. On both occasions he was working from contemporary texts by distinguished writers and he was also quite deliberately submitting himself to work in which he would have to draw on the dark side of his personality. With both rôles however he was fleshing out characters who had been created by dramatists and conceived in theatrical terms. What this meant was that rhetoric and broad gesture could be used and that strong positive emotions like anger were there to act as a scaffolding for the performance. Edward Albee's *Who's Afraid of Virginia Woolf* had been hailed as the best American play of the decade and most critics were to be very happy with Mike Nichols' screen version although many of them were acutely embarrassed by the quesiton of whether what was on the screen was not so much the husband and wife planned by the playwright but rather a bulletin on the marriage of the two stars. It was essentially Miss Taylor's film with Burton there very much in support, but what he did he did quite brilliantly. At last he was playing the don he had always wanted to be but now his urbanity is merely residual for cynicism and self-contempt have drained away all earlier enthusiasms. As Taylor does her thing as the wife Martha she is observed, goaded and yet still accepted by a husband George who is not, as Manny Farber noted, quite the mediocre and reflective spouse envisaged by Albee. He is something far stronger and more complex and what that is essentially is Burton himself forming a core around which the action can take place. Here for Stanley Kauffmann was an actor who had become "a kind a specialist in sensitive self-disgust" and who in this film sailed with "regret and compulsive amusement" on the "great lake of nausea" that was within him. The fascination of this play, especially as filmed, is that it tantalisingly keeps one on that line where brutal psychological realism always threatens to subside totally into grotesque and macabre comedy. Left to Miss Taylor, as Farber suggests, the effect would have been almost *Grand Guignol* but we are kept firmly within the realm of the real world and this never ceases to be the home of an actual New England academic. That this should be so is because Burton was very familiar with both physical and emotional territory and he gauged beautifully how much charm and wit were required. For Crowther he offered "a wonderfully subtle blend of sensitive concern and sadism". Mr Albee and Miss Taylor had nicely allowed him to balance his own acceptance and anger.

In general Peter Shaffer's play *Equus* made its impact on the stage because of John Dexter's brilliant staging. At the time many

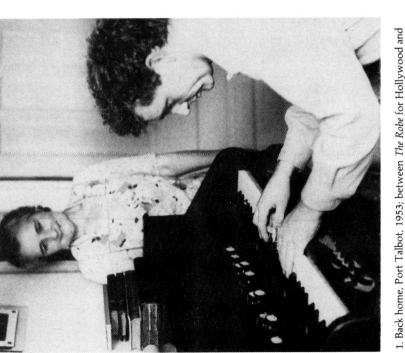

1. Back home, Port Talbot, 1953; between *The Robe* for Hollywood and *Hamlet* for the Old Vic, Burton visits his sister Cecilia (Cissie)

2. *Hamlet*, Old Vic, 1953

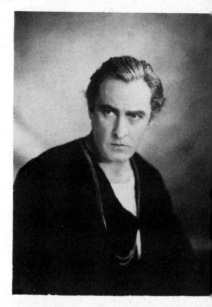

3–6. Laurence Olivier, the Hamlet turned movie idol; John Barrymore, "the greatest Hamlet"; Stanley Baker, a "bloody Welshman"; Burton's New York Hamlet (1964)

7. A striking Coriolanus at the Old Vic, 1952–53 season

8. The first film: *The Last Days of Dolwyn* (1948) with Emlyn Williams

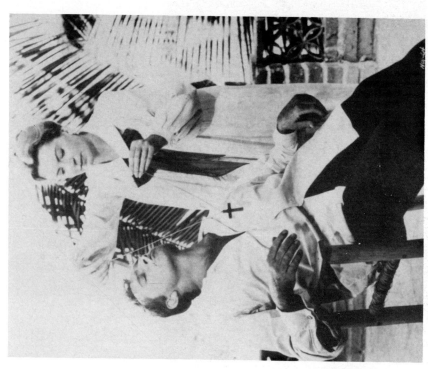

9 & 10. Handsome and angry as Jimmy Porter in *Look Back in Anger* (1959) and the

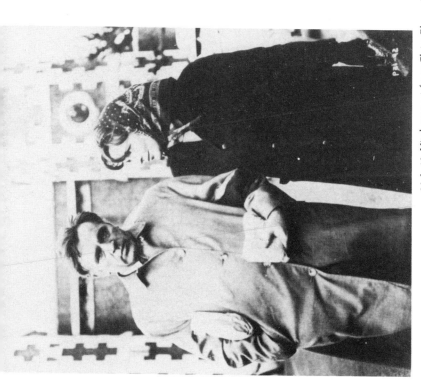

11 & 12. Vital support from Claire Bloom in *The Spy Who Came In From the Cold* (1966); type-cast, the World War II soldier: *Where Eagles Dare* (1969)

13 & 14. A don of sorts: taking a tutorial at Oxford, and back in south Wales at the home of his neice in Cwmafan.

15 & 16. Conspicuous consumption: the Burtons come to London for Elizabeth to visit her first grandchild in 1971, and back to work in *The Assassination of Trotsky* (1972)

people found the psychiatric dimension in the text rather obvious and shallow. By depicting the horses and their blinding realistically rather than stylistically as on the stage the film loses much of the story's intensity but the effect is, as Vincent Canby spotted, to throw far more of the emphasis on to the rôle of the psychoanalyst Martin Dysart, whose rôle in the drama is to wonder at the sheer power of the young delinquent's neuroses even as he realises the extent of his own emptiness and of modern society's general blandness and hypocrisy. Canby was now to be greatly impressed by the film's "serious appraisal of psychiatry" but in this respect he was surely wrong. *Equus* remains a quite startling theatrical experience when staged in its original form but there is just not enough text completely to sustain it as a serious comment on either the violence of youth or the mid-life crisis of a professional mental-health specialist. Burton looks haunted and uncomfortable in the part and once more we are reminded of how impossible it would ever have been for him to have had a career playing contemporary suburban types. He was never born to sit in front-rooms, to prepare salads in modern kitchens or even to open bottles of beaujolais. There is an incredible self-consciousness in all his actions and soon we suspect that he is just waiting for the final declamation which is why he wanted to play the part in the first place. His role, in Canby's words, is that of a "self-mocking, troubled, still-searching miracle worker" but it is only when he latches on to an angry preacher's shouting at God that he really comes to terms with the part. He has to escape from the contemporary settings and retreat into his own private chapel before he becomes fully himself. We wish then, as we were to do so often, that he was in a different and a better film.

In Hollywood they always knew that it was only the camera that revealed who the stars would be. Somebody as ordinary looking as a Fred Austerlitz or a Norma-Jean Baker would produce on film pure images of style and beauty. Over and over again the camera tells us that Richard Burton was wrong for films. A royal head and peasant's body always made him something of an exotic. Alexander Walker greatly valued his depiction of a Kray-like gangster in *Villain* but in truth he was the last person in the world likely to emerge from a humble London home and he looked absurd in his pork-pie hat. He does the Cockney accent well by clenching his teeth but clearly he is enjoying it too much, his delivery is over-ripe, he is linguistically slumming it, his "bleedin' pigeons" belongs in the music-hall. A few years earlier he had conscientiously attempted to be the hard-done-by spy Leamas but he was too intelligent and too posh for the part: as he describes how a prisoner's clothes are returned, "as if they had been sanctified by the Archbishop of Canterbury", he slips into the words of the marriage ceremony and suggests all too readily that he is that archbishop. When he denounces the morality of the Cold War he does so in the tones of a prime minister reflecting over a brandy in the privacy of his study, and when his verdict on a top Russian spy is that "he's a bhaarstad" he becomes a senior foreign-office type commenting on an unprincipled third-world tyrant. Even in his very best films there was always to be some aspect of his appearance and delivery that irritated. Early on the theatre critics had noted his melancholy and also his wide mask-like face which as Audrey Williamson very smartly noted tended not to change throughout a performance. Film demanded a lightness and a speed of emotional response that he could never offer. His only chance was to have worked with writers and directors who would respect his love of language, his intelligence, his sadness and his essentially public or political persona. Somewhere there were priests, academics, soldiers and statesmen that he was born to play but there was something in his nature and in the bad timing of his career that never allowed the right circumstances to occur. He knew perfectly well what the matter was but opted for the easy course of accepting the fame and fortune that bad movies could bring. Such guaranteed rewards permitted and confirmed his sense of his being a personality and meant that there was never a need for him to work seriously and continuously at defining a meaningful cinematic identity.

III
A Public
and Private Affair

III
A Public
and Private Affair

During the course of the 1960s Richard Burton had become as famous as anybody else in the world but as the decade closed it was apparent that he was irritating and annoying far more people than he was pleasing. His intended purchase of a million dollar diamond at Cartier's aroused tremendous interest but so angered *The New York Times* that in an editorial they condemned both Burton and the public for proving in an 'Age of Vulgarity' it was yet possible "to scale the heights of true vulgarity". Just a little later *Time*, a magazine that had so wanted to celebrate the Sixties and to trace its various energies, had little difficulty and probably much support in identifying Burton and his wife as among "the world's prize bores". He had never been idolised in the press but at least earlier reporting had reflected his genuine popularity first amongst the intelligent young theatre-goers of the 1950s and then with all those for whom his depiction of Jimmy Porter had promised a way forward from political and cultural stultification. As the Sixties turned into the Seventies however it was clear that a censorious press was reflecting a wider dissatisfaction and displeasure with the way in which Burton and Elizabeth Taylor were living their lives. They had become thought of as rather charmless and tiresome characters constituting a long-running and rather bad joke.

It is now a commonplace of the History of Our Time that Burton's life was to be transformed by his affair with Elizabeth

Taylor which began during the making of the film *Cleopatra*. American capitalism had always been by its very nature a rather hit-or-miss process and it was always true that Hollywood, which was capable of quietly, cheaply and efficiently producing routine films of enormous style and charm, could also occasionally make disastrous judgements, could totally mislead the normally cautious Wall Street financiers and end up with a complete and utter catastrophe. These gigantic miscalculations usually came at a time of panic when Hollywood feared that it was losing its public and so undoubtedly *Cleopatra*, at $40 million dollars the most expensive film made until that time, was the product of a studio system that had really lost track of its audience in the television age. Shooting was to be plagued by technical and personal problems but underlying all the thinking of Twentieth-Century Fox and Wall Street was the notion that the combination of a well-known and intellectually approved story, exotic and sexy settings and costumes and star names would bring back millions to the cinemas of the world. The end product of four years shooting was not a bad film, but something far worse, a dull one. The movie had its supporters, those like Bosley Crowther who thought it "one of the great epic films of our day" and who particularly liked the acting of Elizabeth Taylor, Rex Harrison and of Burton who was "exciting" as an "arrogant Antony". More typically though and surely more understandably audiences, whilst admiring some set pieces and conceding that the leading players at least looked right, found the whole exercise over-blown and flat with no sharpness either in the action or the dialogue. They had hardly had their money's worth and so there was some sympathy with investors. During its first release, as later, those who viewed the film did so more out of curiosity than out of expectation knowing that the pleasure of the action would be as nothing compared to that of having read about the making of the film. The saga of *Cleopatra* was always to be relished more than the film itself and by far the juiciest aspect of the whole had been the universally appreciated fact of the illicit affair between two of the leading players. Cinema audiences were declining and the patterns of popular culture were changing and Hollywood was much slower than the popular press in realising that in the new age that was dawning there was

considerably more interest in a scandal amongst the internationally famous than there was in a film about a dead Queen of Egypt.

As the Second World War had ended Burton was already
twenty. His fame came in the years of austerity and Cold War
tension that were to follow. At first he was acclaimed by audiences
at the Old Vic and at Stratford and confirmation of what they had
seen and felt was to be found in the review columns and occasionally in the diary pages of morning newspapers and weekend
journals. His name was nationally known but only in a very
restricted way and in a way too that could be carefully controlled.
It was still a world in which one could be as well known as one
wanted to be. There were to be many English classical actors and
even film stars about whom nothing personal would ever be
known and perhaps from the outset there were some who guessed
that the outgoing and rather shocking Welshman would not fit
into that category: he had certainly been given an unique reception
but it was still remarkable how little the general public really knew
about him. He had established his credentials as a leading actor
but the full extent of his charm and his attractiveness were only
really appreciated by those professionals and hangers-on who
constituted the theatrical set and who would meet regularly in
London's bars and restaurants. His voice was becoming increasingly well known because of radio but what he was not and could
not be, because this was still the early 1950s, was what we could
call now a media personality. Television was still a very formal
medium and was still a long way distant from that chat-show
world in which every personality becomes a familiar old friend.
There were good diarists in Fleet Street's middle-brow papers but
that tabloid mentality that feeds solely off the nocturnal activities
of the beautiful people was still a very long way off. Burton could
enjoy himself in public, he could be unfaithful to his Welsh wife
and he could even be just a little outrageous in an innocent
national service sort of way and the only outcome was the mere
suggestion that he was perhaps a little more naughty and a little
more interesting than the usual Stratford type.

Within the popular culture it was thought quite natural that he
would move into films and then as soon as possible on to Hollywood. There was a gnashing of teeth in the Waterloo Road but, of
course, the wider public were far more interested in and aware of

Hollywood than they were of the Old Vic. The final judgement of how good he was, of how right and attractive he was in the parts, would only come in the movies themselves but meanwhile it would be commonly assumed that he would be trying to rip off the studios to the fullest extent and enjoying as many fast cars, swimming pools, cocktails and starlets as the natural laws would allow. Gossip was to Hollywood what electricity was to most other cities and soon the most ardent readers of the columns learned who Burton's friends were and of how active he was on the cocktail circuit. Hollywood had though already learned its lessons and so never took any real risks. We know now that there was an underground Hollywood of crime, vice, drugs and scandal but none of that was ever publicised. The job of the columnists and to a greater extent of the fan magazines and annuals was to suggest a glamorous world in which there were great romances but only ones that sustained a film community based, however short-lived individual marriages were, on the happiness of the star's family. All that glamour, all those shining teeth, thrusting breasts and lovely limbs were the elements of what was assiduously promoted in all press and newsreel publicity as an innocent world. The indication that there were stronger emotions and the hint that this was not just a typical American middle-class suburb was only to be provided in the movies themselves and even then there were strict conventions. Burton could return and personally boast to friends about the lotus-eating life but for the wider public the only crucial evidence that he was having a good time was that on the big screen and it was to be found there in the look of absolute enchantment on the face of Olivia de Havilland as he pinned her to the ground, in the challenging fear in the eyes of Jean Simmons, and in Joan Collins' utter dependence on him in that dinghy scene, although later we were to learn that privately she was one of those who got away. He was just the latest in a long line of handsome young men from nowhere who had gone off to take Hollywood by storm and it was assumed that the rewards of having been born lucky would inevitably accrue. Assumptions were everything; there were nudges and winks as people left the cinema or looked at the publicity stills but that was as far as popular culture would go. The job of the stars was to convey enormous and almost unbearable passion on the screen and to hint at it in their stills but thereafter the conventions drew down the curtain. The whiff of sexual danger was all that was required; for the rest it was to be a case of happy families. Audiences were denied the real anguish and stars were left to salvage what genuine family stability and peace of mind they could surrounded as they were by employers and colleagues who were not really interested in that kind of detail.

In January 1962 Richard Burton arrived on the set of *Cleopatra* to film his scenes with Elizabeth Taylor. In the course of things there had to be some torrid, horizontal, cheek-by-jowl moments in the heavily dramatic and time-honoured Hollywood way. Almost immediately observers began to sense the crackle of real passion and to suspect that the scenes were not suffering from under-re-hearsal. In the past there must have been many film crews who had been through similar experiences but with *Cleopatra* there were probably one or two present who suspected that they were not only witnessing true passion but the making of cultural history. It was quite a bombshell that this leading man who was assumed to be happily married was risking an affair with a film star whose private life had been more closely followed than any-body else's in the history of the medium and not least because of a dramatic pattern of events over the last four years which had included the tragic death of her third husband, a fourth marriage to a television singer, and a death-threatening bout of pneumonia that had held up shooting on *Cleopatra* to such an extent that cast changes were needed.

This was dynamite but it only became so quite so quickly because *Cleopatra* was being filmed not in Hollywood nor even London but in Rome, and of course because this was now the 1960s. Even more than Los Angeles, Rome thrived on gossip and here not only did the Hollywood studio constraints not apply but there were now the burgeoning *paparazzi* not only ready to furnish proof of long looks and held hands but to educate the world into knowing that it now required slightly stronger material than the old film magazines had provided. They were creating the lucra-tive and stylish new art-form of photo-journalistic gossip. Philip Larkin was to claim that "sexual intercourse began in 1963" but it was a year earlier that the world's mass audience of film fans and gossip-column readers first faced up to the fact that the pin-ups who appeared in the fan magazines really did have sex with people other than their spouses. The mystique surrounding fornication was slipping. A couple of years earlier in London a court case had highlighted the fact that characters in novels really did have sex and that same city was soon to have a scandal that revealed anew the extent to which illicit sex was a highly organised activity in contemporary metropolitan life. Naked breasts were occasionally seen in continental fims and underwear began to appear in English-language films. A decade was emerging that was to be more concerned with the explicit revelation and analysis of sex than any that had gone before. Burton and Taylor had played a significant part in opening the new age because they had happened to fall in love in almost exceptionally public circumstances. As they extricated themselves from their standing family commitments and came together as the Burtons they could hardly be surprised or disappointed that a press corps and a readership that had been given so much entertainment by their coming together and which felt so much part of their relationship would want to stick with them to see how things turned out.

The soap opera that was the Burton-Taylor relationship had begun in 1962 and was to run throughout their two periods of marriage and right down to his death in 1984 when she quite effortlessly, and not-at-all surprisingly, became the centre of attention as she mourned a husband who had subsequently had two other wives. The world had followed their every move and in particular had come to expect the ostentatious celebration of birthdays and the buying of magnificent presents. They were, of course, a kind of royalty. Probably there was somewhere a country as real as Monaco of which they were the rulers. Soon audiences were identifying the various brothers, sisters, children and famous friends who became the entourage on public occasions. Curiosity about the Burtons there was always to be but there was very little affection in this worldwide interest and at a fairly early stage there were signs of impatience. Clearly the 1960s seemed to want glamorous personalities and, whereas earlier generations of movie-goers had been quite content to see their favourite starlets smiling beside the pool, now those families and young people who were themselves experiencing affluence and new degrees of social and sexual freedom really wanted to know that those who had

74

succeeded big were living in an outrageously extravagant manner. Beverly Hills was now old-hat. What readers wanted to hear about were Swiss bank accounts, private jets, the world's most expensive jewellery, Mediterranean and Caribbean retreats and all-night parties. The Burtons were seen to be amongst the leaders in this new international party-going world yet on reflection it seems surprising that this was so for, in truth, they were an unlikely pair to be the leaders of a new jet-setting era and it was this unlikeliness or unsuitability for the role that really caused the general feeling of irritation that their mounting publicity occasioned.

They were behaving as if they were royalty and yet unlike some of those who were now to appear regularly in the glossy European magazines, they were not the real thing. There was, though, just the suspicion that they might at least have taken themselves in. He had made his name playing kings, he looked like a natural leader, he wanted to play famous men and be photographed with them, and all his utterances were made as if to the history books. Always there was the suggestion that his wealth and his very obvious enjoyment of it was allowing him to believe that he really was an internationlly important figure. And she, of course, had always been Hollywood's princess, the most beautiful of the studios' young ladies and one who had grown up not so much to be an actress nor a crude pin-up but an important woman in her own right, drawing on both her uniquely stunning beauty and English and artistic background to achieve a real independence. Neither of them was conventionally attractive but both had grown up with stunning physical attributes and both had been led to rely on appeal that was quite distinct from their acting talent or social circumstances. Physically they were very much of the same type, dark and exotic in ways neither fully understood: in him she had recognised something of herself whilst he saw in her his favourite sister as well as semblances of his two most passionately recalled mistresses. They each believed they were special and then the confirmation had mutually occurred when they came together as Antony and Cleopatra. They had the most remarkable eyes of their generation and now those eyes were only for each other they were assured of their status as a new and truly international royalty. In Rome the world had seen all this happening and was happy to go along with the notion that here was a dynastic event. This was however an illusion, a game that could not last for the make-believe prince and princess did not have the charm, talent, or physical resources to make that so.

The rich, as we know, are different and they can also be very boring unless they have something to recommend them other than their conspicuous consumption. That something can be history, style, class, taste, entrepreneurial flair or real political power. The Burtons had none of these things and that was what all the publicity they received in the 1960s tended to accentuate. What was most crucial in this respect was the dichotomy between their regal publicity and their lesser roles as film stars. They were only rich because they had been working actors and the films had clearly become subsidiary now that publicity had really taken over. In his case in particular it was widely appreciated that he had turned his back on what had made him famous and he was now reported to be earning huge sums of money for inferior films, in which he was often miscast and in which, as we have seen, he was in very great danger of breaching those conventions which allow audiences to accept fictional characters as being real within their films. Early on there was a general suspicion that he was no longer a truly professional actor and so all his wealth and ostentation became that much less acceptable. There is very little evidence in either the Sixties or the Seventies that those who read the newspapers thought badly about great wealth and its obvious enjoyment but the public never lost its respect for and expectation of professionalism and as far as public entertainers were concerned almost all kinds of behaviour were tolerated if they were seen to be good. With Burton the story was that of a public losing interest in him as an actor and yet having to go on dealing with him as a personality. In the absence of great films he needed to compensate his public in some other way but he seemed not to have the inclination to do that in any sustained manner.

With Elizabeth Taylor the situation was a little different. A whole generation of movie-goers had grown up with her and, as was the way in those days, had come to feel as familiar with her face, voice and still photographs as if she were a personal friend or even a member of the family. Her familiarity always elicited a variety of responses. There were some who were always afraid of her, perhaps even hated her because of her confidence, her darkness, her knowingness, her irritatingly metallic voice and above all because she was that sexually threatening thing, the adult child who would have no need of an adolescence. More common was a response in which she was not sexually admired as were so many starlets, she was always thought to be too intelligent and abrasive for that, but admired rather for her strongly positive presence in any rôle. With each film there was certainly a fascination with how stunning she would look but also there was an expectancy of a tension that she alone could generate. As film-goers watched her grow up so there developed a respect for precisely that quality in her that Burton never cultivated in himself, for she was indeed a true professional. It was accepted that she was not a great actress, certainly not a natural one and that was usually the quality that most fans wanted in their stars; but she was perhaps a real person who was faced with the prospect of channelling her exceptional looks and undisguisable voice and temperament, not to say temper, into the roles that came her way.

We have had to wait until much later for such excellent studies as that by Brenda Maddox in which the details of Miss Taylor's upbringing have been spelt out, but to a remarkable degree film audiences had suspected the truth. They knew her to be something of a chiseller, someone who had been made into a princess by the studios and her mother, but who had now to make her own living as best she could. She was uniquely beautiful but she was nevertheless a well-known type; there were many college girls and suburban housewives who had that dark intensity and somewhat excessive femininity and who had to come to terms with the constraints of everyday adult life. Everything about her was understood and it was this coupled with her familiarity that ensured her a considerable degree of sympathy and admiration throughout her career. What one was given in any film was usually just another version of her own personality but at least she could always be seen to be trying. There was always something brave about her work whereas he was someone squandering natural talent having run away from the great challenges that his chosen profession offered. Her professional courage genuinely sustained an interest in her as a legitimate film actress for she never breached that unwritten contract with her audiences. That remained as much the case in the post-Burton years as it had from her earliest days.

What really doomed the Burtons as far as their acceptability and popularity as royalty was concerned was their failure to carry over what love and fascination they had for each other in real life into the movies themselves. Their joint ventures were ill-conceived and mediocre and immediately identified as convenient vehicles for them inherently less newsworthy than the reality of their last party. Inevitably those films would be thought of by critics and audiences alike as sheer commercial opportunism and so there was an added obligation for the two stars to breathe into them some life of their own so that they could at least appear to have had some natural artistic justification. Above all the films needed to sustain the notion that the Burtons themselves were naturally charming and interesting people. They just about got away with *The VIPs* which was a worthy enough story and which had the feel of absolute verisimilitude as if it had been made almost as a documentary as they were passing through the airport. Thereafter there was always something unsatisfactory about their joint appearances, for either the story was banal or their mere presence so crushed the story as to make it meaningless. Early on the evidence suggested that it would be difficult to bring their acting styles together in anything that could be termed a pleasing film. They had come together with the setting of epic romance but contemporary romance and comedy, let alone any of the traditional genre, seemed out of the question. There was to be one exception, of course, one film in which the story was strong enouqh to bear the weight of their presence and in which they could both at the outset be accepted as professional actors making film work. The trouble with *Who's Afraid of Virginia Woolf* though was that the film was an exhausting emotional experience to sit through and that as it progressed one began to feel more and more as if one had been let into a real-life domestic scene. Here was the final proof that the Burtons were not really glamorous royals but rather a somewhat tiresome and disreputable suburban couple. What they had needed in the 1960s was just one hint of charm or class in an intelligently directed movie.

What was really against the Burtons was time for now they were being expected to sustain the role as glamorous people even as the odds were stacking up against them. Brenda Maddox has firmly and clearly made the point that Liz Taylor was a movie star very much in the Fifties mould; it was families that had gone to the cinema to see her films and who bought those film albums in which her portraits were nearly always the most memorable feature. Burton had never looked quite right in those same albums but he too was essentially a man of the early Fifties who had made his impact as a representative of a youth that would offer an exotic and physical challenge to the existing middle-class conventions of both stage and film. At the time of their coming together in *Cleopatra* he was thirty-six and she was twenty-eight and in their exotic costumes they could relax in the knowledge that they were where they were because they had been counted amongst the most strikingly handsome people of the decade that had just ended. One needs special qualities to make the onset of middle age attractive to other people and the Burtons were to be deficient in that respect. Nor were they helped by the fact that more rapidly than ever before the standards of what was required by way of physical beauty and star quality were changing. In Rome there had obviously been an enormous degree of mutual physical attraction and as Burton later tried to capture her beauty in words he recalled their first meeting in which she had seemed "the most astonishingly self-contained, pulchritudinous, remote, removed, inaccessible woman I had ever seen" and one with breasts that were "apocalyptic". This last judgement gives the game away with regard both to his tastes and her appeal. He was the soldier of the 1940s who had fallen for a dark beauty whose stunning face was always to be supported first and foremost by the promise of those breasts as suggested by a carefully-controlled cleavage. What was promised was offered to him but never to her audiences for she was never to betray the chaste and puritan standards of those film annuals of the Forties and Fifties. She could only exploit her sexuality in the way that Hollywood had established. That was in part because she had taken on the puritanism that the profession required but increasingly in the 1960s after she had met Burton it was a realist recognition on her part that she was a very different physical type from what was then in fashion. As she grew older so she became, as far as the evidence of the camera was concerned, shorter and stockier. In the era of increasingly topless and long-limbed youngsters she could never be a sex symbol or even a romantic lead. The interest in her was very much that of seeing how any middle-aged housewife would struggle to control her figure. Her professional talents were leading her in the direction of character acting.

It was largely because of her perceptibly changing shape that the Burtons became less and less acceptable as leaders of the glamour set and increasingly the interest was in their comings and goings and in their spending rather than their image. In fact there were those who from the very earliest days of the relationship found it difficult to accept them together on the screen and who held them both responsible for that. *The Sandpiper* which was their third film together did much to finish them off as romantic leads and during a screening of it the critic Pauline Kael heard one man describe them as "pygmies" and another ask "Where's the rest of them?". Miss Kael noted that during the same scene in which Taylor poses topless for a sculptor she cups her breast in her hands to talk to Burton but, reflects the critic, "they seem inadequate to the task". The writing was indeed on the wall. Later the director Peter Bogdanovich was in an audience that tittered with embarrassment when during *The Comedians* Burton suddenly reached over and grabbed Taylor's breast. The audience, said Bogdanovich, had suddenly realised that they were seeing something on film which actually occurred in the privacy of the actors' real lives and so they felt they had been sharply "taken out of the film". The point that he was making was that this could happen in bad films but it was not by accident that he had picked on the Burtons for his main example because all too often they embarrassed in their films because their appearance and behaviour suggested that they were an actual middle-aged couple and so that natural suspension of disbelief that is the essential starting-point for cinema audiences did not occur. Whatever their private passions they were not good for each other on screen. Any notion that they were exciting people could not possibly survive the banality of their output. They were the stars now only of the gossip they generated.

The decline of Richard Burton is almost always discussed in this context of his relationship with Elizabeth Taylor and this was most noticeably the case in Melvyn Bragg's major biography. For Bragg the chief point about Taylor was the total artificiality of the world she had always inhabited; she was a child of the studios and the gossip columns and quite obviously the post-*Cleopatra* period of glamour was for her but the last chapter in a career of blazing publicity. His argument is that there could never be any "normality" in her life, "there never had been and there never could be" for "she was as pinned to her public stardom as a traditionally trapped suburban house-wife to her kitchen". In this analysis the falling in love with Taylor and the decision to end the marriage with his Welsh wife and to marry her was the crucial and fatal turning-point in Burton's life. The dangers of this step were fully appreciated both by Burton's closest British friends and his family and so Bragg is able to emphasise that he was well and truly warned. Nevertheless passion took its course and Burton took, what was, for Bragg, the great "gamble" that made him essentially a "renegade" against his family, his Welshness and the natural line of succession in the hierarchy of great actors. In what was to become a lengthy study Bragg is anxious to make the most of this great point of no return, this burning of the boats, and so he begins to draw on his full literary power in order to understand the force that so fully diverted and captured his hero. At one point Miss Taylor was a "privileged English heiress" (*sic.*), suitable plunder for a "Celtic marauder", but later she became Burton's "true" and "unexplored America". The very obvious parallel with Shakespeare's Antony and Cleopatra was irresistible and Bragg stresses the part played by "sexual lust" and Taylor's hypnotic powers in turning this new Antony away from the serious matters in Rome. Ultimately, though, Bragg retreats into his favourite novelist's trick to capture the full impact of this critical juncture as he argues that when "Burton began his move towards Taylor, he was leaving the well-built fortress of his adult ambitions to go back into the no-man's-land of adolescent dreams".

Bragg leaves almost no metaphor untouched as he searches for the language that will explain the "dotage of his general" and not surprisingly these over-written pages constitute the weakest section of his book. It was a dramatic moment in Burton's life but in an attempt to do it justice Bragg seems to have succumbed to prejudices and a special-pleading that are not characteristic of other sections of his study. What he cannot deny, of course, is the degree of natural physical attraction and the real sense of adven-

ture that Miss Taylor promised. Writing more or less at the same
time as Bragg but dealing with this moment more succinctly and
sympathetically Graham Jenkins just contrasts the security offered within his brother's first marriage as compared to the "unpredictable and dangerous excitment" offered now by this new
affair. Having accepted the inevitability of that first attraction
Jenkins then moves on very quickly to make the point that Elizabeth Taylor possessed one great gift as far as Burton was concerned and that was her ability to lift him "out of his deep moods
of depression". For all the temptation to lapse into the language
of trashy romance or even of Shakespeare's Octavius Caesar when
describing what happened during and after the filming of *Cleopatra* we have really to start with the fact that two adults came
together at the start of a marriage that was to be remarkably
successful by show-business standards and in which there was to
be good deal of natural dependence. At the point where he is
trying to explain the all-embracing nature of Miss Taylor's victory
Bragg makes a comment that more fully than anything else that
has been written conveys the basis of the successful relationship
between the Burtons. He remarks on how they had "become a
unit, a republic of two, increasingly a law and a state on their
own". Something like that occurs in many successful marriages
and it must be something that other people will envy even if they
are aware of its danger. We can understand how it can happen
when the partners are equal in their passions and in their intelligence, when they are both committed to professional careers,
and when their financial expectations and preferences force them
to live in a somewhat artificial exile. What should concern us here
is why it was that Burton entered that republic and what was its
relationship to his own decline?

The most extraordinary instance of Bragg's special pleading is
the notion that the man who went to Rome to play Antony was
securely established within "the well-built fortress of his adult
ambitions". The truth, as Graham Jenkins far more accurately
conveyed, was that Burton was very much at a crisis point. He was
already a tax exile with a home in Switzerland and yet having
essentially removed himself from the London theatre scene he had
failed to establish a clear identity in Hollywood. He had no obvious professional base upon which to build and yet already he

was fully committed to enjoying the riches he could earn. His marriage to Sybil had never prevented serious affairs and in New York he had almost left her for Susan Strasberg. Meanwhile the dreadful truth had dawned that his second daughter was schizophrenic and autistic. Already he was an exceptionally heavy drinker and one, the evidence suggests, who found it impossible to do his job without alcoholic support. By the end of 1961 he would appear to be a man ripe for some kind of diversion or alternatively, of course, some kind of help. So far he had progressed from challenge to challenge always sure of his ability to succeed. The only slight turning-back had come when he first returned from Hollywood to play at the Old Vic, but certainly in 1961 it was already too late for any dramatic renunciation of life-style. Necessarily his immediate family was no longer a safe haven and that prevented any possibility of a retreat into a quieter domestic or even professional life in Switzerland or London. As always he trusted his instincts, he followed the dictates of his talent, he accepted the opportunities that success created, he went on enjoying the pleasurable consequences of being wealthy. He was ripe for a new adventure, for a new set of circumstances, and what was crucial was that in the new relationship there could indeed be a considerable confirmation and reassurance of things in and about himself. In the sexual stakes there was confirmation of his appeal and his performance. There was a marvellous snubbing of Hollywood where he had never fitted in and had never really understood the nature of their craft. Now he had captured their greatest star who also happened to be one of their great professionals. Above all though the confirmation that he really needed was that which concerned the way in which life should be lived. The man who married Elizabeth Taylor did not think of himself as someone who was turning his back on or destroying what was most important in his life but rather as one who was receiving the ultimate assurance that those things which really mattered could indeed become almost the sole basis of one's existence. What he most valued and enjoyed in himself was his capacity to talk and laugh even as he ate and drank. This was the life for which he now opted.

In his life success had come because of his own remarkable qualities. Now there was to be a daily confirmation and celebra-

tion of those qualities and all that was most brilliant and original
about him would be on display as he and his wife talked about art
or literature, gossiped, rubbed shoulders with the worlds's most
powerful and beautiful people, and, over the very best food and
wine, planned the spending of their absurd but thoroughly
deserved wealth. Everything that was boring and unnecessary
had been eliminated from their life together and so their sense of
triumph was total. They chose their own settings and their preference was for Switzerland, the Dorchester, and Puerto Vallarta.
Naturally they had effective control over the company they kept
and so the game was always played on their terms. Money was
earned easily enough and always in ways that conformed with
their togetherness and their routines. There was no need of any
outside buttressing, for everything that they required could be
provided for by their own resources. Both the child of the studios
and the Welsh orphan had found a true home and one that was
based on all that they respected. It is not difficult to see what
someone brought up in Los Angeles would find attractive in the
identity offered by Jewishness and as Bragg has commented Burton's Welshness was but an extension of the Judaism she had
embraced. His earlier grand passions indicate that he too was
drawn to Jewishness and in the marriage of these two stars there
did seem both at the outset and later a kind of tribal, peasant
legitimacy. For Burton his Welshness was something in which he
never ceased to glory and yet it was never an affectation nor
something that had to be proved. It could always be taken for
granted even if it had to be commented on daily. What was crucial
though was that it only needed to be occasionally sought in Wales
itself for wherever he went he took Wales with him. The name of
his Swiss home, Pays de Galles, applied really to all his ports of
extended call. That sense of Wales was always with him and its
celebration within his marriage or with visiting friends was just
about the most pleasurable thing in his life. The same was true
really of both theatre and literature. He had triumphed in the
former and the memories of that were far more valuable than the
need to find any further meaning or praise in new productions.
As for books the joy was in owning them, in suddenly checking
quotes, and in giving constant proof to family and visitors alike
that they had been read and remembered. If Burton had been lured

into a marriage it was one in which he was being asked to emphasise all the things he liked best about himself. In what possible way was he endangering either his talent or his values?

The Burtons became dull, boring and irritating in the 1960s rather in the way that often happens to those people who are given such a special place within a marriage that they never have to prove it to the outside world. Their drama, their sense of importance, their essential meaning had all been determined privately and they had no real need of wider approval as Burton in particular insisted on showing in many of his films. It was infuriating for the public to be given any glimpses of those aspects of the relationship that they really wanted to see. Instinctively one knew that one was not seeing the best of either of them in terms of their conversation or their acting. The biographies of Burton are littered with references to his absolute genius as a conversationalist and story teller; that was undoubtedly what he did best of all and yet how many of us were ever allowed the privilege of spending a whole evening or even a meal time with the man? There would be story after story about his Welsh family, about the London stage and Hollywood with the whole performance accompanied by utterly convincing impersonations of both the humble and the high and mighty not to mention quotations from Dylan Thomas and whole Shakespearean speeches. Andreas Teuber who was Mephistopheles to both his Oxford and film Faustus has talked about his absolute mastery of the story-telling art, the way in which anecdotes were used as gnomic devices quite replacing the need for any philosophical analysis of the issue at hand. Teuber's view now is that justice could only be done to the memory of Burton by splicing together the clips of all the chat-shows on which he ever appeared and even then much of the spontaneity and informality of the real thing would be lost, not to mention the warmth that came when he was operating with a true friend and equal like his brother Ifor when the medium would be Welsh as much as English. Who can doubt that this was Burton's métier and yet whilst suspecting this the public of the 1960s and 1970s were never admitted to it. The Burtons had become private performers and not surprisingly their audiences felt cheated. The last thing actors should ever do is to convey the impression that their domestic life is more interesting and demanding than their public one. In this respect as in several others Burton just ignored the pact that should exist between a star and his public.

Everything that had ever happened to Burton had suggested to him that he possessed special qualities and now he had been given very direct confirmation of that. Ultimately however there would be need for him to give the world and posterity some final proof of his greatness that could be judged outside of his family circle. It would have to be something outside of acting for increasingly all the dreams of returning to London to head the National Theatre and to play Lear could not be reconciled with his boredom with acting and his need to drink when he acted. What he had to do, of course, was to write. Everything had pointed in that direction; his love of verse, his admiration of Dylan Thomas, his short stay at Oxford and his greatness as a raconteur. Above all there was the way in which, almost by accident, he had established a lifestyle and a timetable that essentially was that of a best-selling writer. To read accounts of the Burton marriage is to be taken into a world that has best been described in countless literary biographies; the exotic locations, the casual visitors, the family crises, the booze and yet the sense of isolation and intensity are all preparing for the masterpiece. If ever things had been set up for the great Welsh novel then they were at Céligny and Puerto Vallarta. Burton knew that. He was fully aware that it was only by writing the great book that he would really justify the lifestyle that he had achieved and prove to himself that his intellectual and physical sense of his own meaningfulless was legitimate. He talked a lot about writing and he did write, articles, short books, a stab at a novel and a diary. None of this amounted to greatness and there was nothing to challenge the view that he was far more involved with the notion of being a writer than he was a great writer just waiting for the idea that would ensure a masterpiece.

In the diary extracts that Bragg has reproduced one begins to understand that the only possible subject that Burton could ever write about was that of Elizabeth and himself. Their wealth, their passion and their sense of being special had cut them off from what for most people constituted political and cultural reality and to a far greater extent than usual they had become the leading players in their own drama. For whatever complex psychological and physiological reason she had become the star of a drama based on her own body and to live with her was to be caught up in an epic in which death or some grotesque and disturbing ailment was a daily possibility. The cultivation of beauty had quickly lapsed into a battle against flab and then a gambling with death. In his case too the body that had guaranteed fame, but which in truth had always been rather troublesome, now established its own priorities and above all they were to concern drink. As was the way with many of those acting colleagues whose company had had enjoyed most and writers whose works he most wanted to quote he became an alcoholic. There were so many reasons to drink, it had been an activity always at the core of his marriage and perhaps indeed it was needed to soothe both the ache of so many family tragedies involving death, injury and disability and the physical inadequacy of a body that was arthritic, epileptic, acneed, haemophiliac and ageing. At first he would have drunk because it was the best guarantee of that warmth and spontaneity that good company should always seek but then later he must have found that it was drink that brought on the best stories, the best performances and the fullest sense of his rhetoric having some resonance. Early on his income from routine films and then his marriage to Elizabeth Taylor had sheltered him from the need actually to prove his greatness publicly but left now with only the memory that he had been a great Coriolanus and Hamlet and with the fact that he was only the star in his own family life it was drinking that became the best guarantor of approval. In his later years there was always to be a pretentious and overblown quality about his public ventures whether they related to his idea of being a great Lear, an outstanding don, a producer of great television or even as the obvious man to play any great historical contemporary figure and it is not difficult to see the influence of drink at work in sustaining the notion that he must be great and culturally relevant. Alcoholics create their own sense of what is possible and naturally they become incomprehensible and boring to a public that needs confirmation of greatness on its own terms.

Elizabeth Taylor and drink allowed Burton to sustain the notion of his greatness and to enjoy a sense of power for many years after those things had been seriously tested in the public arena. His lifestyle was that of a tycoon or of the president of a banana republic and yet it was also one which necessarily always impinged on entertainment and the arts. His very appearance and his public image cried out for statement, for relevant statement that is or significance. His qualities had set up that kind of expectation, and yet he was only an actor who had once been seen in Shakespeare and since then in one or two good films. He had been lucky in that his natural gifts had allowed him instant success and then the luxury in which to go on celebrating his own good fortune. All the time though both he and his public had to live with the desperately frustrating fact that if the words were not by Shakespeare or from the Bible then the message could never be as challenging and profound as was promised by that noble head, that saint's face and those sadly knowing eyes.

Burton and Taylor: the names will always go together as naturally as in the advertising slogan that was popular in their early lives. Inevitably his partnership with her will rather eclipse the many other chapters of his long complicated love life and even perhaps the memory of that marital musical chairs which came in his later years. He was generally very lucky with his women and certainly he married four remarkable women each of whom gave him a great deal and whom he very much loved. Initially Elizabeth's arrival had estranged Philip Burton and members of the family but soon she, like his other wives, was accepted as a natural and fully rewarding addition to Richard's life. It was his good fortune that Sybil had given him the secure base from which to launch his incursion into an alien metropolitan world and at the end he was incredibly blessed with a wife, Sally, who not only encouraged him to secure a final plateau of artistic achievement but who subsequently set out to organise and secure his posthumous reputation. Set alongside his other wives and passions the unavoidable conclusion must be that Elizabeth Taylor created the circumstances in which he ruined himself physically but he was ripe for that experience and it is difficult to detect what defences he had against it. Try as we may it is impossible to see him living in Brighton and commuting Olivier-style to the National Theatre. Miss Taylor clinched it but he had already gone a long way to committing himself to performing the only rôle that he could enjoy and that made sense, that of being Richard Burton.

IV
"Bloody Welshman"

IV

"Bloody Welshman"

That phrase was most memorably uttered at the end of Joseph Losey's 1962 film *Eve*. The words were spoken in St Mark's Square, Venice, by Eve herself, a high-class tart played by Jeanne Moreau, and were directed at Tyvian Jones, a pathetic former lover who had come to the Venice Biennale masquerading as the author of a highly-acclaimed novel which in fact had been written by a recently deceased coal-mining brother. The wretchedly weak and opportunistic Jones was magnificently played by Stanley Baker, an actor who on other occasions when he was not starring in baroque studies of corruption would have been the proud and amused recipient of that epithet and of others like it. Baker and his colleague and friend Richard Burton were always to be "bloody Welshmen", aware at moments of triumph and failure that they were different and that they would always be seen to be different. Above all they would be different when amongst the English who, knowing that they were Welsh, would expect things of them by way of amusement and vitality. In addition there would always be a tension, one based in part on jealousy and in part on distrust. Both of them had first lived among the English during the Second World War, a time when the need for national solidarity saw the old Evelyn Waugh view of the Welsh as being "feckless and unemployable" give way to the notion that some of their more positive features could be used to enrich the quality of national life. Thereafter there was always a tendency to retain a certain English ambivalence to the Welsh and as both Baker and Burton became international stars and moved in the frequently bland world of film studios and expensive hotels then their own sure sense of Welsh identity was both envied and suspected. The responses of strangers always threw them back on their sense of themselves. Things were complicated further by their being entertainers: they had to assume many parts but perhaps it was only when asserting or contemplating their Welshness that they were fully happy with themselves. Ultimately they could not escape their understanding of themselves as "bloody Welshmen" and that was a matter of choice and of pride. Perhaps too it was something of a limitation.

In 1976 Burton was greatly shocked to hear that Baker had died of cancer at the age of forty-eight, and of his own volition rushed off an obituary to the *Observer*. It is a confused and probably drunken piece of writing in which the predominant tone is that of anger. "What thieves these dead men are" is the lament of someone who had been cheated of the expected satisfaction of dying first. Very frequently grief is self-pity and Bragg reasonably assumes that on this occasion Burton had been plunged back into the sense of loss and guilt associated with the earlier death of his brother Ifor. There was also, though, the guilt that came now with the full realisation of a love and regard for his friend which had never been fully understood or expressed whilst he was alive. Even today it is not easy to read this somewhat confused, nakedly honest and utterly selfish account of Burton's grief and torment. It is a genuinely embarrassing essay and not least because quite remarkably the author makes no reference at all to the fact that the recently knighted Sir Stanley Baker was by trade an actor. Nothing in the whole of Burton's career so fully revealed the extent to which he never thought of himself as belonging to a profession as his failure in this obituary to refer to the fact that his dead friend had been a distinguished actor, a far more effective screen actor than he was himself, and in addition a successful producer. Certainly Burton was jealous of the other's artistic success and more especially of the knighthood, but surely there was some obligation on him at this point to express some admiration at what Baker had achieved by taking film seriously. Rather his concern was to identify his friend as a fellow-countryman and in doing so mourn the loss of one who belonged to that small group of internationally famous Welshmen. "There are so few of us" is the central strand in his thinking, "so few of us" compared to the English, so few of us that nobody can be spared. All the time the memory of his friend is driving him towards social definition. What he really wants to talk about is the fact that "there is a class of Welshmen, original and unique to themselves, powerful and loud and dangerous and clever". These people "are almost all South Walians" and it is this essential point of both him and Baker being South Walian that Burton wants now to contemplate and investigate as he sits alone by his typewriter in Los Angeles.

What he wants to commemorate and celebrate is that "tremendous thrill of vitality" that he associates with those successful people that share his background and that he thinks is to be found at its most developed in those who came from the Rhondda Valley. The names that spring to his mind are those of actor Donald Houston, the novelist Gwyn Thomas and the rugby players Cliff Morgan and Bleddyn Williams. The first two were certainly Rhondda men but technically the sportsmen had grown up in adjacent valleys. With Stanley, of course, there had been no doubt for "he was the authentic dark voice of the Rhondda Valley", a man "inwrought with his valley" to the same extent as Burton now thinks of himself as being inwrought with "the idea of the valley". Clearly what he is doing here is concurring with that popular notion that took the Rhondda Valley, or more accurately the Rhondda Valleys, as the paradigm of all Welsh mining communities. The Rhondda was indeed a classic case and justifiably famous; it had staged the most bitter strikes, it was the birthplace of the union and then of that militancy that had so shaken England, its chapels were the biggest, its choirs and bands the best and so were its sportsmen, especially and quite crucially its boxers. Everything that was typical of and most worthwhile in the urban civilisation that was South Wales was to be found in the Rhondda and other South Walians accepted its international reputation and were prepared like Burton to concede that they came from a slightly lesser version of it. In both Rhondda Valleys there were uninterrupted strings of genuine towns and that provided an intensity and a richness of activity that no other valley could fully match.

Burton himself had been born in what was by comparison an

almost rural setting. His rather isolated home had stood by a stream in the narrowest of all valleys and at the end of a village which even more than most seemed to have come to terms with the local topography in only the most arbitary and perilous way. Whilst still a young child he had been taken to live with his sister and he was to grow up in a very different kind of village, one on the edge of a coastal town: he was really not 'a valley boy' at all but rather one who had lived near that Welsh industrial town most cruelly exposed to the Atlantic winds and gales. But his village was a mining village and that, as far as Burton was concerned, was the heart of the matter. He, Baker and his other heroes were the products of a coalfield and it was that fact which had ensured that their values would always be democratic, their politics radical, their attitude to the establishment and to the English that of disrespect, their attachment to their family total and their belief in their own superiority absolute.

The miners were, in the words of the cliché, a breed apart but more than that they were quite simply the men who did the most demanding, the most unnatural, the most dangerous and the most vitally important work in the whole of industrial society. That situation might or might not be internationally recognised but it was certainly the case in Britain where there was the further realisation that Welsh miners, and especially those who lived in or near the Rhondda, were the natural aristocrats and leaders of the proletariat. Like many workers in demanding and successful industries the miners took enormous pride in their sheer professionalism but added to that there was a sense of physical prowess, of solidarity and of economic importance which made them feel special and which communicated itself to the families and to communities that depended on their efforts. Loyalties emanated outwards from that sense of shared superiority and significance which was created at the mine and there was a deep intensification of the normal working-class attachment to family, to chapel and to sporting heroes. 'The valley', the idea of which Burton found so central to his thinking, was indeed a vital image for geography had played its part in South Wales, cutting mining communities off from other industries both by distance and topography. The miners did indeed live alone within remarkably limited horizons and foreshortened days. Of no other manual workers was so much demanded but at least miners lived in communities which they could readily dominate by acting together in the way in which they had been trained both in the pit and by the union. The nature of the industry and of the landscape did much to explain both the informality of the community and the refusal to take non-miners seriously. These things explained too a quite absolute familiarity: there could be no secrets and from the place of work would come the cruel jokes and nicknames that would instantly encapsulate whatever affectation or eccentricity any individual had assumed. Families remained close even after rows but so too did neighbours and friends; the community really was a kind of extended family and certainly workmates were essentially brothers. This was precisely the way that Burton thought of Stanley Baker. Miners were naturally gregarious but there was also a suspicion of outsiders and at least twice in his obituary Burton was to refer to Baker's difficulties with other people. The fact was "he did not like people very much" and this distrust it is suggested amounted to "paranoia". All of this quite naturally had made dear the friendship and loyalty of one's own kind.

The pride always expressed itself in terms of community and friendship but quite basic to the sense of identity was coal itself. You were a hanger-on, a second-class citizen unless you could establish your direct relationship with the real stuff. You had to be party to the talk of prices, of conditions, of the assessment of overlookers and management, you had to be part of the routine, part of that daily schedule of providing food, clothes and hot water, you had to have experienced both the pride in achievement and the tragedy of death, accident and ill-health. "Nobody knows except us" says Burton as he recalls how Stanley Baker had grown up in grinding poverty in the shadow of the pit where his father had long ago lost a leg. For Burton himself by far the most important thing about his own father was that he had been a respected coalface worker. He was a rascal, a drunkard, a short terrier of a man but down in the pit he was a champion and that was all that mattered. The son was to remember him as someone absolutely entitled to talk about the coalface with all the affection and expertise with which other men talked about women. Then there were his other male relations who had become more important in his life after the death of his mother; Elfed, the brother-in-law in whose home he lived was another greatly respected miner as was Ifor, the brother who in effect became head of the family as well as Richard's closest and most valued companion. Men like this stood at the summit of a culture based on coal and to grow up respecting them was to take on a set of standards and values that would leave one rather unimpressed by alternative claims of authority. It was a culture in which there was an immediate relationship between work and physique and miners and their families were always aware of what the job demanded, of what kind of build and strength were needed and necessarily individuals became self-conscious of their own attributes. Miners lived on very close terms with their bodies and so too did those who grew up in miners' homes. As actors both Baker and Burton were forced to develop that total body awareness that was needed just as much in the very different profession they had chosen but they were always helped by a pride in their bodies and a sense of them that had been developed in a previous dispensation. It was the miner in Baker that Burton most wanted to remember, a "tallish, thickish" man "with a face like a determined fist prepared to take the first blow but not the second". He knew full well that he was not that tough himself, that he was, in a phrase that he used in describing his last rugby game, "the soft-cover, paper-back edition" of their "hard volumes", and yet his fondest boast was that he was his father's son and as such he was in possession of a body that for all its limitations would withstand the pressures of work, neglect and abuse.

Miners were certainly suspicious of outsiders and rather given to patronising them but within their home communities they always accepted the fact that only the fittest were suitable for and could survive underground. They favoured industrial and political solidarity but nevertheless fully expected and even encouraged degrees of vocational pluralism. There was considerable social mobility within the industry itself, there was a clear ladder of promotion and improvement and nobody was more respected than the working miner who had secured a manager's certificate. Meanwhile the community needed shopkeepers, shop-assistants, clerks, publicans, carpenters, undertakers and even policemen and in these respects the dictates of nature and family circumstances were accepted. The appropriate personnel would always

be recruited on the basis of their mental and physical attributes or
within the conventions that allowed the youngest child to be given
the chance to escape the pit and the children of the recently
bereaved to make whatever arrangement economic survival required. If one was destined to be a shop-assistant then that was
accepted however much that fate would initially strike those
youngsters like Burton who had to go through it as a total humil-
iation. Furthermore there was a special joy for mining comunities
in the encouragement of those of their number who had special
talents and skills, for it was hoped that the successful, especially
if they escaped the valley, would always remember their roots and
would even allow great pride and pleasure to be taken in their
achievements. The identification of potential and the nurturing of
skills were carefully entrusted to the various agencies that came
to characterise every town and village. Primarily this was the
function of schools but with so many children forced to leave at
an early age, many of them after only a tantalisingly short time in
grammar schools, there was an urgent need for organisations that
would allow a second chance and that in effect became the rôle of
the chapels, of evening classes, of correspondence courses and in
time of youth clubs. All the while the local cultural and recre-
ational scene was being enriched by mass participation but to a
remarkable extent the South Wales coalfield loved competition
and it had developed into a fine art the process of encouraging the
emergence of champions, of winners, and to use the term that was
applied to the most charismatic ministers of religion, of stars.

Necessarily within this culture and this process teachers played
a crucial role. They stood alongside ministers as a group that was
very much part of the community and yet one that was expected
to stand a little way back from it in order to protect its special
mystique. In both cases there was no absolute standard; some
ministers would baffle, some would entertain whilst others would
console and guide. With teachers there would be many who were
merely workhorses, there were others who were particularly good
at encouraging pupils to pass exams and win competitions whilst
there were some with special gifts of personality and scholarship
who were admired for bringing distinction to the community. The
idea that state education had been developed since 1870 merely
to develop a workforce that could understand orders had never

satisfied the Welsh and so it was that by the time of the First World War nearly every urban and rural community had both elementary schools in which there were masters specialising in identifying pupils suitable for secondary education and an access to secondary schools in which there were degreed teachers capable of work that compared to anything that was done in public schools or even indeed in the universities themselves. The English had constructed a class-based system of education that allowed for some mobility but the Welsh, aware of their past deficiencies and eager to exploit the newly publicly financed opportunities, soon fashioned a link between elementary and secondary education that was unique within the kingdom and which thus allowed a larger proportion of working-class children to experience academic courses than was generally the case. It was not necessarily common sense that prevailed in this matter for there was no attempt to relate secondary education to the industrial needs of the area by developing technical courses, it being assumed that vocational and commercial courses were best left to private academies. What mattered most was that Wales could be shown to have schools that were as academic and as competitive as those in England and that a small number of genuine scholars would emerge. Necessarily in this process a very large percentage of pupils left school at the age of fourteen or fifteen to become clerks or shop-assistants but they did so having been introduced to the subjects and topics they might have studied at university if only they could have hung on for a few more years. Quite simply the fact was that a significantly large minority of Welsh working-class children most of whom were under fifteen were being given an education that would in a later era be perfectly acceptable at undergraduate level within an American state university. These pupils developed a special affection for the History, the Mathematics, the Languages and above all the Literature and the Poetry that they were taught. An affection developed too for those teachers who whilst insisting on the passing of exams nevertheless had the time and the inclination to reveal the magic and the sanctity of the printed word.

Just the thought of Stanley Baker was sufficient to remind Richard Burton of how much they were both products of a very distinctive society and one with highly developed cultural conventions. He had grown up in a coalfield which above all else respected the capacity of men to work and yet one in which conflict and recession all too often brought unemployment. Individual fortunes varied but when there was ready cash and any opportunity no effort was spared to treat and even spoil children and especially the youngest amongst them. It was a proud industrial society utterly familiar with the way in which misfortune and privilege went hand in hand. There would be many tragedies but it was readily accepted that the best compensation was to make sure that those who were special were protected and favoured. Burton had started life as Richard Jenkins and had been born to a drunken father and a mother who died when he was two. But then there were brothers and sisters to take him in, to spoil him, to ensure that he would not go unloved, and to encourage him to be different and better. His special place within the family (he was the twelfth of thirteen children) made it very likely that he would be among those groomed for secondary education but even then there had to be those alert and sensitive teachers to spot his potential. In the event he became one of the privileged few who not only went to a good secondary school but who stayed on to gain the school certificate and the possibility of higher education. He did this, though, in a way that was doubly remarkable and which illustrated quite perfectly the extent to which a mining community was poised to assist its proteges. On the eve of his taking his school certificate circumstances had forced him to take a job in the local Co-op haberdashery department. Yet within eighteen months a network of teachers, youth-club leaders and politicians had negotiated his return to school, and then soon after an identity of interests which had been established in school and radio drama productions and the A.T.C. resulted in his being taken in as a ward of the community's most talented teacher.

Philip Burton had himself been born into a Welsh mining family and could take his own experience in gaining a degree as an example of what could be achieved even in the most unpromising of circumstances. He had achieved a position of respect and trust as a teacher but he knew that he had special gifts which were as yet unfulfilled. His plays were produced both locally and on Welsh radio and he was convinced that his flair and passion for drama would bring further fame both to himself and to those talented pupils of his like Owen Jones who had gone from Port Talbot to London's West End. The care of the Jenkins family and the subsequent talent-spotting of local teachers had made the young Richard well aware of his own potential and it was that fact which smoothed the path for Philip Burton's take-over. Now, as he metamorphosed into Richard Burton, the youngster was placing himself in the care of a man determined to make a mark and one who was fascinated by the whole question of how much a Welsh miner's son had to change in order to become accepted in the cultural circles of the English. In his play *Granton Street* written almost ten years before the young Richard moved into his lodgings, Philip Burton had written about a working-class family that had to come to terms with one of its number whom college had allowed to become a member of "a new cultured class" but who was not able to forget that he was a miner's son. That clearly autobiographical play had been written by a man who had benefited from personal and social energies that had yet not been fully released, someone who yearned to see a coming together of all that was best in the English and Welsh cultural traditions and for whom that meant in particular the English language on the one hand and Welsh dramatic intensity on the other.

Ultimately in South Wales the talented were expected to find their own metier but initially that did not prevent the youngsters from being all-rounders. There was nothing to stop the young scholar from being a boy-preacher, an instrumentalist, a soloist or a rugby player. Alun Richards has written quite beautifully in several of his books and not least in his biography of Carwyn James, of the ways in which small Welsh grammar schools could nurture all the talents and were especially delighted to find a genuine all-rounder in true Renaissance or at least public school style. Richard Jenkins was one such all-rounder whom different teachers might have developed in rather different ways but Philip Burton had alighted on Drama as the vehicle for both his own talents and those of his pupils. In some ways this was somewhat surprising given his own academic qualifications in Mathematics and History and given also the relative lack of a tradition in South Wales where a chapel-dominated culture had rather frowned on theatre which it associated with not entirely respectable showmen. In fact things had been changing rapidly and building on the popularity of professional theatre in Cardiff and Swansea and a growing interest in drama in the Welsh university colleges a new passion for amateur dramatics was actually sweeping across the South Wales coalfield. In the severe depression of the 1930s it was undoubtedly true that chapel-based activities lost out to new cultural groups and schoolteachers really began to replace ministers as the arbiters of what was legitimate and fashionable. The leaders of the revival in drama benefitted greatly from the fact that so many young people were unemployed or at least were not entirely exhausted by the unsatisfactory jobs that were available and at the same time their efforts were being given both stimulation and opportunities by the development of Welsh regional broadcasting. Their pupils, of course, were not entirely raw for long experience of school and local eisteddfodau and also of public speaking within the chapels would have given them a certain inherent theatricality. It had always been a society that valued both participation and entertainment and now at last drama could take its place as a respectable activity no longer the preserve of touring players. Philip Burton was a pioneer in helping to establish a new dimension within the culture, one that could be diverting and instructive both for audiences and players but also one that could take up remarkable indigenous qualities that were as yet neglected.

With Richard Jenkins he had much to build on. He was, of course, a very striking youth, not conventionally pretty but one with a real sense of presence that developed out of the way in which a peasant sturdiness was rounded off with that noble head. The Celtic darkness and quickness obviously came from the coal-mining father as did the roundness of the face but there was undoubtedly a mystery ingredient in his make up that might well have come from the Jewish grandparent whom nobody ever mentions but of whom he was always later to boast. Certainly in Welsh terms there was something a little exotic about every member of the large Jenkins family; all the brothers and sisters were physically impressive and stylish and several of them were very striking indeed. It was Richard though who stood out. Everything about him suggested intelligence and there was something remarkable about the head and face, especially those green and what were later described as visionary eyes. The young boy had always recited at the chapel and at school in both the languages commonly used at home and in the village and for his family too he had preached his own sermons. He was obviously a natural for Philip Burton's school productions and then as the closer relationship developed so the teacher could see the greater possibilities. In acting terms the relatively straightforward task was that of teaching him to use his natural attributes so as to create a sense of controlled power or of what all the critics later came to describe as 'stillness'. Meanwhile the greater challenge was with the voice and this was a matter about which Philip Burton had particularly strong views. This was largely a matter of his own upbringing for as someone who had been brought up in a Welsh valley by English parents he knew that not all South Walians spoke in the same way, and in his play *Granton Street* the directions made it quite clear that his family were to speak in accents "far removed from that of stage-Welshmen" and there was to be "no exaggerated rolling of r's and hissing of s's". They were to speak "just plain English". Most Welsh families could never manage to speak in that way but at least they knew that those of their children who went to grammar schools would lose the worst aspects of their accent and would come to speak with a far more acceptable cultured Welsh accent that would be good enough for college, the ministry, the bank and office-work generally. All grammar-school teachers were elocutionists of a sort but obviously the teachers of English and Drama felt a special responsibility for those pupils who had natural voices that might be useful in public life.

Philip Burton was proud of being English but even more his life had come to revolve around activities like drama, the Anglican church and the air squadron where the English language needed to be spoken in very special ways. What his experience of the Cardiff and London stage and more especially the B.B.C. had taught him was that certain Welshmen had the capacity to speak or rather to perform the English language in a way that was more pleasing, varied, subtle and meaningful than the English and especially the southern English themselves. The secret was to take the confidence, passion and enthusiasm that the chapel had encouraged as well as the freshness that came with those who were in effect learning a second and essentially public language and to add to that something of the formality and authority required by

Anglicans, airmen and radio producers. For a year and half the renamed Richard Burton lived with his mentor and was trained for his school certificate and to speak English in such a way that would make him a natural actor, priest or broadcaster. This second aspect of his training was to give him what was to be by far his most important qualification. Working with the Psalms and Shakespeare his mentor had trained him to use his Welsh voice to speak English verse beautifully and precisely and it was that ability which allowed him, courtesy of the B.B.C., the A.T.C. and Oxford University, to establish himself on the bottom rung of the English acting profession.

In his obituary of Stanley Baker, Burton was trying hard to work out what it was that made them South Walian blood-brothers but all the while he was also nagging away at those things which made him different and which might well have caused a tension between them that is certainly implied but never admitted. He quickly makes the obvious points concerning his friend's greater dislike of strangers, his unease with people generally and his physical robustness but what obviously worries him more is the fact that he is going to have to make it clear to readers that "lovely old Stanley wasn't exactly cultured". Burton concedes that this is a "murderous" point to make in an obituary and he correctly anticipated that it would offend Lady Baker, but then, in contradiction of himself, he goes on to cite three or four instances in which his dead friend had suddenly surprised him by coming up with apt literary quotations, by his ability to explain the meaning of "In the beginning was the Word" and by his sudden recognition of William Faulkner whom they had met during a drunken night in Spain. When finally he makes the comparison between the anger of Baker and that of the poet R.S. Thomas one takes the point that he has laboured to make, that his friend was a more intelligent and a better-read Welshman than many outsiders may have realised. Nevertheless the overall impact is still one of rather patronising condescension on Burton's part. What the essayist is really saying is that we, the readers, would have expected him, Burton, actually to have known all those things for himself and whilst on these occasions he had been pre-empted or upstaged it remained true in general terms that it was he who was the more cultured of the two. He was fully aware of Baker's career and of how similar it was to his own; he knew in particular that his friend had also been 'found' by a local school-teacher, who had encouraged his acting talents, worked on his accent and eventually written plays for him. What Burton could not forget though was that Baker had come from a much poorer background, was far more genuinely proletarian and that at his secondary school he had received a far less academic training and then had left to work in an electrical factory. Without making any reference to the profession of acting he chooses to lament the passing of his friend by trying to suggest both by his anecdotes, by his style and by his assumptions of what his readers would already know that his own Welshness and his own more general fame were essentially related to his greater degree of cultural and intellectual attainment.

Richard Burton was indeed an intelligent and cultured man but he was those things very largely because of the resources available in and the encouragement given by a small Welsh town in the early years of the Second World War. He had been educated to school certificate level in seven subjects and given a special feel for the finest English verse by a gifted local teacher and playwright. Thereafter he was to receive no formal academic training other than those summer courses at Oxford which many people were later to misinterpret as a full undergraduate education. He was product of a community whose religious and educational traditions prompted intelligent youngsters to develop a respect for good writing and in particular to go in search of that meaning and significance that could only be found in the public performance of literature and especially verse. It was a society in which those with a certain degree of native wit and flair were inevitably drawn into certain literary and performance traditions. To a remarkable degree his passions, curriculum and critical framework were all determined in his Port Talbot years and although subsequently he would be stimulated into further reading by book reviews and dinner-table suggestions there would be no revolutionary breakthrough in cultural terms. The basic reference points were always to be the Bible, Shakespeare and the local poet Dylan Thomas who had lived just ten miles away around the bay and who was another Welshman who had received all his education within the confines of a grammar school where he too had been drawn to the power of a formally spoken and intoned

English. Burton always retained his essentially schoolboy passions for the great standards of the Eng. Lit. curriculum and in the absence of a higher education his great enthusiasm for the new literary discoveries that he made was always that of the adult education student. Certainly he loved reading and sharing his new passions at the dinner table or in the bar but in general there was a strangely isolated and private quality about his love-affair with books which meant that his literary side was always a matter of personal retreat and confirmation rather than professional or scholarly engagement. This of course is precisely the rôle that literature plays in the lives of the vast majority of readers but with Burton what could have been merely a matter of personal inclination inevitably became caught up in the wider questions of his public image and of his public and cultural significance.

The man who could publicly conclude that "lovely old Stanley was not exactly cultured" was someone who throughout his career had cultivated the satisfying notions that he was a scholar manqué and that if financial circumstances would allow there was always the option of an academic career. There were always to be those Oxford contacts who on their occasional visits would help to sustain his notion that the transfer to academe could be easily accomplished but deep down he knew the difficulties and must have realised the extent to which his fantasies reflected the disappointment of opportunities lost rather than concrete possibilities. The library at Céligny looked for all the world like the room of an Oxford don but it was always a compensation for what might have been rather than the launching-pad of any new career. His contemplation of literature was essentially a private or conversational matter and the difficulties of making it anything more than that were always to be very evident on those almost embarrassing occasion when Burton allowed his personal enthusiasms to become public ventures. There was that notorious New York occasion in 1964 when Burton and Taylor took part in an evening of poetry reading directed by Philip Burton and organised to raise funds for his ailing theatre academy. "Barely has poetry drawn such a crowd" reflected the *New York Times* critic as he surveyed the gathering of fashionable Manhattanites but although Burton himself was to score some successes, those present were left to reflect on what at times had been a "banal" selection and to determine for themselves what the evening was really meant to signify. Because his ventures were always personal and inspired by his own enthusiasms rather than by any collective intellectual consideration they were nearly always to seem to objective critics to be rather old-fashioned, somewhat pretentious, a little shambolic and certainly not fully thought out. He always proceeded as if his own interest and commitment were enough to guarantee scholastic and intellectual significance. It was always a question of just bringing together a couple of his mates rather then submitting himself to any settled academic or professionl context. The zest of the schoolboy had lingered on but in isolation it retained all of its innocence even as it took on new dimensions of arrogance and ignorance. How else can we explain the absolutely horrific pretentiousness and awfulness of the film in which he intended to pay homage to the verse of Christopher Marlowe and then later the rather feeble contributions to the output of H.T.V., the television station of which he had become a director? Away from Céligny, British and American academic and cultural life had moved on, there were new fashions in poetry and in how it should be read and there were new movements and standards in both film and television production. Quite simply Burton stood apart from so much of contemporary academic and artistic life and remained at heart the impressionable and eager schoolboy.

Given his life of exile and of general dependence on crudely commercial films then the only area in which there could be any meaningful personal development was that of his own writing. Essentially he became trapped in a position in which he just had to write to justify his own sense of his worth and the expectations of respected friends. Everything was drawing him towards his desk and his typewriter and yet this great student of English verse and Dylan Thomas enthusiast did not feel inspired to write verse and neither did the classical actor in him feel any impulse towards emulating the playwriting of his mentor. Rather his love of anecdote and cherished memories of childhood and youth drew him towards prose and the art of story-telling. In this respect he was clearly following the dictates of his own abilities but equally he was again revealing the extent to which he was a product of a particular culture. His lifetime was to coincide almost precisely with the flowering of a distinctive regional literature, a literature that he admired and that was always to shape his own style and taste. Quite naturally he felt that if he were to be a prose writer then other Anglo-Welsh writers were already creating the idiom within which he should work. The poetry of Dylan Thomas became the most internationally acclaimed accomplishment of Anglo-Welsh writing in these years and for Burton it always constituted the kind of excellence that he and other aspiring Welsh writers should seek to emulate. The poetry itself of course could not be emulated for it was seen as the one-off product of a rare and untypical genius. More relevant was Thomas's prose writing which was always distinguished but which could quite clearly be related to a wider tradition of short-story-telling that was becoming characteristic of a society in which grammar-school trained writers were attempting to reflect the uniqueness of a vibrant urban society which spoke two languages and which seemed so close to the peasant and Christian past even as it strived after everything new that popular culture and especially Hollywood had to offer. Thomas even more than Burton was a townsman but in his prose he beautifully recalled that blend of the urban and peasant that was so much a part of the memories of so many Welsh families in the first half of the century. Burton's own *A Christmas Story* was obviously his tribute to Thomas just as his published journalism was a nod in the direction of his other hero Gwyn Thomas, the novelist whose love of American fiction and films had led him all the more to appreciate the comic potential of a South Wales where overnight a peasant labour force had stumbled into an awareness of the great social questions of the era. Burton knew who his masters were but after very briefly venturing into the areas they had opened up he was to retreat in the knowledge that he was not really in that league. His notebooks became the testing-ground in which he searched for what the subject of his literary endeavours should really be.

Throughout his career Burton lived with the notion that he was really an Anglo-Welsh intellectual. He might not have the original poetic talent of Dylan Thomas but he knew far more about Welsh industrial society and his great theatrical success had allowed him to achieve an urbanity and a set of contacts and of friends that encouraged his sense of his own significance. As he went on reading, building up his library, and sharpening his powers of observation and expression in his notebooks there was some recognition of how far he had travelled from the community to which his favoured literary style was so closely related but perhaps there was less understanding of those accidents and quirks of fate in his own career which had prevented his full academic development. He was never able to comprehend fully the extent to which that distinctive culture of which he was a product had set him up as it were with certain talents and enthusiasms, had given him in the favourite phrase of schoolteachers 'a good grounding' upon which it had been his adult responsibilty to build. For a very complicated variety of reasons that subsequent intellectual development had not occurred. Quite remarkable success in certain activities that carried a high degree of artistic and social distinction prevented many people and certainly himself from fully realising that in so many respects he remained the promising undeveloped person that he had been as a school-leaver. It was only as he continually expressed his dissatisfaction and lack of respect for the acting profession that we see him moving towards his understanding of the fact that his great success, fame and wealth had come through activities that were not absolutely essential to the development of a potential Anglo-Welsh intellectual and yet without those things he really would have remained a nothing. He wanted to be so much more than what his actual talents had led him to be. Remarkable as those talents were they had not been enough really to satisfy.

Initially he had made that vital breakthrough out of his town because of his voice. He first came to the notice of a wider audience because of the beauty with which he spoke the English language. His potential in that respect had been noted by a mentor who throughout his life had been angered by the assumption that all South Walians spoke in the stereotype of early Anglo-Welsh writing and the music hall. As we have seen it was Philip Burton's own English heritage and then his exposure to the Anglican Church, to the University, the Air Force and the B.B.C. that had developed his appreciation of well-spoken English and in his capacity as a teacher he became convinced that Welsh boys brought up in a tradition that prompted the more extrovert of them into dramatic renditions of well-known texts could be trained to switch languages and to become exciting exponents of the language of

Shakespeare. Richard's voice was the product of his guardian's theory, preoccupation, expertise and rigorously applied instruction. For the young student the public enunciation of difficult and yet mellifluous verse that had been written in a language that was at once alien and tantalisingly familiar became itself the very process of self-fulfilment and discovery as well as the precise measure of educational advance. The *raison d'être* of Welsh secondary schools had become the channelling of a talented élite into professions that were dominated by standards of attainment and behaviour that were set in England, and of course each profession had its own demands in terms of qualificaiton and periods of training. As it happened Burton had been brought to a level of excellence in an area of expertise which the local culture was capable of recognising instantly. How easy it was for a talented youth to become a broadcaster when his mentor had direct access to the studios of a B.B.C. region that was particularly anxious to encourage the performance of new verse and drama. How easy too for a teacher who was well known as a playwright and broadcaster subsequently to direct his protégé towards a successful Welsh actor-manager who had already begun to interest English provincial and metropolitan audiences in Anglo-Welsh themes. Richard Burton entered public life smoothly and swiftly and did so essentially as the possessor of a lovely voice.

It was from his base as a broadcaster that Burton was to launch his national career. His speaking voice became known through the auspices of a B.B.C. that was prepared and indeed eager to encourage regional identities within the national culture and as part of that was continually on the look out for new writing and performing talent. This was precisely the same B.B.C. that helped to confirm Dylan Thomas's sense of his own worth above all by encouraging him to complete his highly innovative play for voices *Under Milk Wood* which was in 1954 to give Burton his most famous and widely-acclaimed radio rôle. As much as anything else in the culture it was the B.B.C. which confirmed as being utterly realistic the dreams of schoolteachers that their pupils could win unprecedented acclaim and which breathed new confidence into almost every aspect of Anglo-Welsh literary and intellectual endeavour. In that decade after 1945 it was B.B.C. sponsorship which confirmed that the new writing was not parochial, that its idioms were not only of regional or comic interest and that Welshness was adding something to the possibilities of broadcast English. Burton entered into public prominence as part of a process in which a regional culture as a whole was sensing a new legitimacy, a new distinction and vast new possibilities. His own voice was very much his ticket of entry into a wider world and perhaps it was always to remain that aspect of his public self that people would best remember. His major stage rôles were not filmed and given the general quality of his commercial films it is perhaps inevitably the quality of his voice that remains his most significant legacy to subsequent generations. Melvyn Bragg has carefully itemised his quite considerable sound archive and it is one from which one could imagine many people wanting to choose extracts for any sojourn on a desert island. It remains a remarkable and powerful voice but one that was very much a product of its time and circumstances.

In the 1940s and 1950s the national radio audience was to hear more and more of what was termed 'the cultured Welsh voice' as it became generally appreciated that it was adding greatly to the range of broadcast sound at a time when most regional English accents and not least that of London itself were unacceptable. The Welsh were to become announcers, presenters and readers although it was in the dramatic possibilities of their voices that most interest was shown. There was a range of possibilities as any comparison with Burton's contemporaries reveals. Dylan Thomas's voice became one of the most distinctive in the land: it was Welsh and yet there was nothing plebeian about it; it was the voice of a bourgeois, a refined observer struck by the follies and foibles of all those with whom he had come into contact since his earliest years, a confident voice sure in its judgements and the precision of its vocabulary, a voice intended to entertain and boomed out so as to reach all listeners but never one humbly seeking approval, for its prose was rooted in a sure sense of social standing and its poetry the product of an imagination that never doubted the coherence and flow of its language. It was Emlyn Williams who took Dylan's prose down the social scale and made it more peasant and parochial, often annoyingly emphasising precisely the comic aspects of Welsh place-names and pronunciations that English audiences would have been accustomed to in the music hall and in radio comedy but nevertheless using his theatrical effeminacy and camp fussiness to underline precisely the slightly precious and rather feminine superiority and precision of the author's standpoint. Of course Emlyn could speak 'posh' as well as anyone but that too seemed very much part of his essentially satirical armoury. For his young pupil Philip Burton had a very different voice in mind; it was to be one trained specifically to speak Shakespeare and so it needed to avoid all hints of affectation, eccentricity and the comic. In a way it needed to be a far more conventional voice, one far more socially acceptable and yet still capable of conveying a Celtic power.

Burton's voice was a highly distinctive one and few people who have heard it will have difficulty in recalling its wonderful precision, clarity and firmness. To listen to the Burton archive however is to be a little surprised for it emerges that there was certainly more than one way in which the voice could be used. It is easy to forget that there was a restrained and subdued Burton mode which illustrates most fully the extent to which his work with Philip Burton had given him the option of eliminating all trace of Port Talbot and South Wales. When he wanted to he could speak wtih a totally convincing upper-class English accent, one that in its beautiful modulation and exciting depth always hinted at public use but only in a way which would have been regarded as utterly normal in any English university, courtroom, church, boardroom or officers' mess. That voice would have opened the door to any profession but as he uses it in his various recordings of English verse and prose it becomes increasingly clear that it was an instrument that had been developed with his career as an actor very much in mind. Its versatility is almost as astonishing as its sheer Englishness. There are times when reading the verse of Donne that he sounds as if he could be any one of half a dozen English romantic film stars from Pinewood or Elstree studios. With other lyrical poems he sounds for all the world exactly like his friend and colleague John Neville who was perhaps the finest and clearest reader of English verse, and there are other occasions when he clearly seeks to give his voice the clean metallic quality of Olivier. He could do the English then in many different voices, all of them utterly acceptable both in the professional and theatrical worlds of that southern English culture that was thought of as setting the standards for the rest of the country. In terms of his own professional career it is essential to realise the extent to which his vocal training had been aimed at making him one of the most impressive speakers of English within the accepted social and artistic conventions of his day. Nevertheless in his own view of himself his astonishing success at speaking English so beautifully was never seen as an opportunity to abandon his background by attempting to integrate but rather came as confirmation of how special had been that background and of how easily his own gifts could bring rewards.

That urbane and so utterly English Burton is not the one that most people would recall and would want to remember. What far more readily comes to mind is either the heroic Burton or the Anglo-Welsh Burton reading his beloved Thomas. The heroic Burton was that marvellous young actor who took both London and Stratford by storm in part because of the enormous dramatic power with which he speaks Shakespearean verse. What was so thrilling about that voice was its sheer masculinity and enthusiasm, here was a strong and active young man confident of his athletic prowess and also of his vocal range. The timbre of the voice celebrated the language and conveyed to the listeners a confidence that allowed them to commit themselves to it as it went in search of meaning. The Burton sound that so excited theatregoers in the early fifties is best preserved in the recording he made of *The Ancient Mariner*, a venture in which he was assisted by his two friends John Neville and Robert Hardy who in their contributions remind us of just how clearly and beautifully English was being spoken by the leading actors of that decade. Burton's job is to sustain the telling of the mariner's tale; he does it quite magnificently and Coleridge's great romantic poem is injected with the very fullest dramatic power. The voice feeds off both the poetic structure and rhyme and the sheer power and pace of the narrative, always gaining strength and yet also having all the range clearly to identify different voices, to colour key words, to isolate the impact of each image and above all genuinely to frighten. What other voice could make the word 'roar' so much of an onomatopoeia and so consistently convey the power of nature? Who else could have so clearly established the individuality of the narrator and so convincingly conveyed the power and mystery and yet utter credibility of this fantastic tale? The voice that loved the telling of the tale was absolutely capable of driving home its terrible and ghastly nature. We fully relive what the mariner had seen and experienced. "O shrieve me, shrieve me, holy man!" entreats Burton as he triumphs in the spell he has wrought and shows us the extent to which he was so completely at home in the great tradition of spoken verse that the educational system had maintained as one of the glories of English culture until that time.

More recently there will have been a far greater familiarity with Burton's various readings of Dylan Thomas and especially his versions of the First Voice in *Under Milk Wood* which he did for radio in 1954 and for a film in 1971. There is no doubt that his performances of Thomas did much to contribute to the poet's popularity but on reflection it would seem that Burton was far from an ideal reader of his friend's work. His renditions of the First Voice's introduction are far too earnest, too formal, too reverential and too churchy to establish the fanciful, poetic and mock-serious tone that the play requires. Too much of Burton's own personality comes into play and we begin to appreciate quite how classical and how English a public performer he was. On another occasion he was to record the famous morning 'hymn' of the Reverend Eli Jenkins (a part read by Philip Burton in the first broadcast) and in his attempt to create a comic stage-Welsh character voice he came out sounding thoroughly Scottish as he rolled his 'r's' in the music hall fashion. To play at being Welsh was now the most difficult thing for him to do, and perhaps it was just as difficult to accept that not all dramatic prose and not all verse which he found to be personally meaningful needed its significance communicated in the same way. The best illustration of this is provided by 'Fern Hill', one of the best known and most widely acclaimed poems written in the Anglo-Welsh tradition and a recording of which many students of modern verse would want to own. Dylan speaks his own poem entirely without affectation and almost entirely without emphasis. He is concerned only with the clear communication of each word and the only element of interpretation discernible is the sustained note of regret for a childhood long since over, a regret that is there from the first line. His only trick is a slowing of the pace as the layers of meaning thicken but there is never any striving after effect or noticeable fear that a listener's attention needs to be regained. Burton could read 'Fern Hill' in that way and was to record a low-key version, but at the *Homage to Dylan Thomas* recorded at the Globe Theatre in 1954 he went for a fully theatrical performance and in so doing revealed so many of his strengths and weaknesses. Far more than Dylan his voice is genuinely boyish and we are immediately introduced to an entirely appropriate mode of youthful enthusiasm: from the start there is a marvellous colouring of key words, the 'o's' in 'golden' and 'lordly' are exquisitely prolonged and the very special and exalted status of the child is marvellously suggested. Of course the child who has become the poet and the speaker was very clever and sensitive but Burton was able here to lapse into authentic South Wales vowel sounds by shortening his 'a's' and the effect is to personalise the recollection and make us believe the experience. All these are gains and something has been added to the poem that one would not want to be without. But suddenly Burton steps up the pace and turns up the volume. Where Dylan slowed so as to let the words do their work, the actor now spurts and shouts and in so doing rather indicates, somewhat in the manner of the musical organ that the voice so resembles, that no other form of emphasis was available. The poet's reflection is melancholic and elegaic; the actor wants to be angry and wants us to know that his anger is of cosmic significance. His grave and portentous tone as he considers what it must have been like "after the birth of the simple light" is a clear announcement that we are entering into a reflection of great historical and religious significance. God we feel was certainly present in that childhood paradise and now the speaker is trying hard to make God hear his voice.

As it was in that reading of 'Fern Hill' so it was very often to be with the voice of Richard Burton, a voice that was loved and admired by many but which never lost its capacity to annoy and irritate others. On occasions he could show that he had all the lyrical and reflective gentleness that so much English verse requires but what he took special pride in was the great power that he could give to dramatic verse and it is in that respect that he both thrilled and gave offence. There were always to be lovely tones and always too the thrill of boyish urgency, that sense of a call to action. It was always a voice of authority, a voice whose commands would at once be obeyed. It was a classic Shakespearean

114

voice, one demanding that kind of certainty and intelligence; it was effortlessly royal and suggested that noble action was at hand. It was quite naturally a priestly voice and one that could equally convey either religious faith or anger and confusion. It was classically a timeless voice that could of its own accord create the dimension of history: it was no wonder that he was drawn to playing statesman and that he was to become the best mimic of Winston Churchill, the statesman who most fully thought of himself as representing the noble tradition of England and who composed and spoke his sentences as if he were addressing History itself. Yet as had happened in 'Fern Hill' there was always the danger with Burton that he would become impatient with the initial pace of what he was speaking and that he would go in search of some meaning that his audience could not share. There would be a surge of power from the lungs, a somewhat equine snorting and a shouting that seemed all too arbitrary. Critics often compared that tendency to shout with the tricks that Olivier had always used but whereas the English actor was always thinking in theatrical terms Burton's change of pace and volume was always part of his attempt to invest some intellectual or spiritual meaning. It was a voice that allowed listeners little rest, it was perhaps over lush for English tastes, too much of a thing in its own right, and certainly too earnest and too serious. It can be heard at its worst in the film of *Dr Faustus* where Burton's physical woodenness and facial deadness are accompanied by a dreadful recital of all his verbal tricks. Emphasis comes only through a curling or a smacking of the lips, through ugly snarls and by occasional spurts as if to relieve a tedium. There is a random lengthening of certain words and a desperate attempt to inject all personal and place names with significance. Latin quotations are very knowingly reeled off with great swank and then rather condescendingly translated. It is a clownish performance in which a voice is striving for effect without having any confidence or interest in the words themselves. It is a voice set in no clear intellectual context.

Richard Burton had been encouraged by a local community to believe that he was in possession of special gifts and then as he had very quickly come to the attention of the English theatrical world he had been given full confirmation of his early promise.

He had fulfilled Philip Burton's dream for at this stage he was beating the English at their own game by speaking their verse better than they did themselves and yet combining with that quality the excitement of an exotic. His thrilling voice gave a deeper resonance to English texts and yet had unmistakably Welsh elements; he looked like a prince and yet his striking apperance was most un-English. To the English stage he had brought a new athleticism and masculinity and yet also a new spirituality. Just as Dylan Thomas had taken London's literary world by storm so now a decade later another South Walian was the rage of Soho and Fitzrovia as he seemed to herald a new era of theatrical glory. Meanwhile in Wales there was enormous pride in his achievement, a pride that focused on how a local culture had identified and trained a talent and on how confirmation had now been given that a society of peasants and workers could produce a young man with precisely the kind of class appreciated in the best English circles. Here indeed was an authentic Anglo-Welsh hero, a distinctive personality certainly and yet so much an amalgam of all the qualities which his fellow countrymen valued most. He seemed the best kind of advertisement for all the agencies and avenues of progress that the Welsh had devised to ensure that the best of the old traditions were successfully blended with what British society as a whole now seemed to require. He was a miner's son proud of his close-knit family, he spoke Welsh, he played rugby, he was in the words of the crucial test very much 'one of the boys' and yet he had also done well at precisely those skills that had become almost the *raison d'être* of chapels and secondary schools. Nothing jarred in his curriculum vitae, he was a model. His success made so many things seem worthwhile, seemed a reward for so much effort that the community had expended, seemed to justify a half century of Welsh history. Above all Richard Burton's success had proved that the mix was right, that a balance had been achieved, for his South Wales had wanted young men to be both religious and secular, both athletes and aesthetes, both loyal to their class and capable of success in their own right. Nobody in Wales doubted that he was Olivier's heir and as one contemplates that fact so one realises that in the England of mid-century no other actor could have made claim to that title with quite the degree of support from a whole community. At home he had done well in the way that Wales expected and now as a Welshman he had succeeded in England.

Eventually he was to fail and that failure was to be deeply felt in Wales. Of course he went on passing some of the old tests: he was good to his Welsh relatives, he turned up at rugby matches, he had lots of Welsh mates, he gave money to good causes, he enjoyed singing and Welsh jokes, he could swear and tell stories in both languages and eventually he was to show an interest in the state of Welsh television. So many loyalties had remained but he was no longer a hero. He had failed because he was no longer the best: he had run away from the challenge and become something of an international laughing-stock on account of his bad films and his bad taste and judgement in allowing his life to be the subject of so much gossip. His erstwhile Welsh admirers could detect the elements of personal tragedy even before they knew the full details of his dependence on drink but what worried them more was the suspicion that his demise was inevitable precisely because he was so Welsh. This seemed as if it were the Dylan Thomas story over again. Why was it that so many Welshmen, in common perhaps with other Celts, were capable of brilliant, early and pioneering successes in those aspects of creativity that the English so admired and yet so abused their talent and their bodies that they quickly burnt out and often died at tragically early ages? To the Celts that think in these terms it is little consolation to point to the very large number of non-Celtic writers and actors whose careers were foreshortened through indiscipline and indulgence, for it is their own heroes whom they care about most and with them the failure always seemed more tragic because the initial success was so uncommon and had been a matter celebrated by communities as a whole. The truth is that such failure is thought to reflect on the community and inevitably leads to a crisis of confidence. It is too easy to believe in John Morgan's memorable dictum: "the Welsh have all the talents, except for being forty-five", too easy to conclude that the Welsh enjoy success and acclaim, want these things to accrue without too much effort being expended, and somehow lack the secret of pacing themselves as well as those other Anglo-Saxon qualities of stamina, patience and organising ability. The pride in Burton gave way to a sense of displeasure. His notoriety became something of an embarrass-

117

ment and all the while there was that nagging thought that he had failed because he was so Welsh. Had he been too spoiled by those brothers and sisters and pushed too hard by that ambitious schoolmaster? Had those triumphs at Stratford and the Old Vic come too easily? Had he been encouraged to believe that Hollywood would just be a push-over? And most worrying of all was the thought that his delight in his Welshness and all his deliberate attempts to remain loyal to so many aspects of his Anglo-Welsh background had not been enough to sustain and save him. Could it be then that his determination to hang on to aspects of his Welshness was an attempt to disguise his failure at developing a clear adult identity and was it further possible that this was a reflection as much on his native culture as on himself?

So salutary was Burton's demise that the Welsh still need to be reassured. Surely it is true that the grammar schools did not just force spectacular yet artificial plants which died once out of the greenhouse. Their great success had been in turning out several generations of well-qualified professionals whose expertise ranged from the competent to the brilliant. Out of the schools came managers, local government officers, civil servants, teachers and academics all of whom served the community and fought to sustain its liberal and human values. At the same time there were others equally professional who went into the arts and became musicians, composers, writers and actors. There was always the suspicion that creativity was closely related to instability for every village had its brilliantly eccentric preachers, teachers and musicians, but Wales must now face up to the fact that it is perfectly capable of producing writers, musicians, broadcasters and even actors and producers who are every bit as stable and professional as their contemporaries who went in for 'nine to five' jobs. In theatrical terms the suicide of Rachel Roberts and the one-time alcoholism of Anthony Hopkins confirmed old fears but the real story has been of a remarkable flowering of talent although so revolutionary have social and cultural changes been since midcentury that individual success is now taken far more for granted, is less widely reported in the popular press and is far less related to wider class and community loyalties. Richard Burton was an Anglo-Welsh icon but now far less thought is given to the Welshness of Anthony Hopkins, say, or of his fellow actors Roger Rees,

Jonathan Pryce and Mike Gwilym, let alone brilliantly successful directors like Peter Gill and Howard Davies.

What is so obvious now is that Welsh artists work in a context, are supported by an infrastructure and are therefore always encouraged to see themselves both as professionals and as collaborators and team-members. What is so reassuring is that the sheer professionalism of all the arts is maintained as such by companies and structures within Wales as in England. There are still some spectacular individual success stories but the emphasis now is far more on sustaining a regular programme of high quality television, music and drama and what both planners, artists and audiences seem to want is the promise of a full calendar of events rather than occasions dominated by star personalities. To contemplate the extent to which audiences now take television drama and films with their astonishingly high standards of acting and production for granted and to review the intensity of musical and artistic life in Cardiff is to realise how greatly things have changed since the early manhood of Richard Burton. In retrospect we can appreciate now the extent to which he was as much a victim as a product of the 1940s. Success came so early and so easily because there were people in Port Talbot who for all their small-town isolation had direct access to broadcasting, to touring companies and to service and educational agencies offering startling opportunities. In national terms his great breakthrough in the 1950s came because the leading theatres were more than anything else crying out for stars to bring new life to Shakespeare's great rôles. Once Stratford and even London were conquered the road to Hollywood was direct. In that ten year period between 1945 and 1955 in which he went from triumph to triumph he knew that he could rely on his initial gifts, his voice, his presence and his ability quickly to learn and adapt as he studied each rôle, but never was he really intellectually challenged or forced to think seriously about the nature of his talent and the ways in which it could be adapted to different kinds of work. He had left Port Talbot secure in the knowledge of his ability and the challenge of life in the wide world was never that of learning new things but rather that of just making the right contacts that would allow him to display his gifts. He would be amongst the English and so his innate charm and charisma would always carry the day, and the people who mattered in the theatre were only producers and directors whose function was to create opportunities for the stars. He became one of the country's most acclaimed actors in what were the last few years before English theatre passed into the hands of writers and directors whose first task was to teach actors a new humility. Similarly he became a film star in the classic Hollywood context in which studio moguls signed up every famous name and good-looking actor and in which nobody had seriously begun to think about the cultural possibilities of the English-language film. In so many ways we keep coming back to Burton as a product of the early 1950s for he was someone instantly granted fame in two spheres of popular culture that yearned for his charisma and yet neither of those spheres was as yet socially or intellectually attuned to the values and energies he had been stimulated by in his youth. He just squeezed in to the last classic years of the old film magazines and albums but by the same token he was just to miss a new wave of film and television production that was totally to transform the culture of his native land. His family and his teachers had told him that he was special, and of course he was, but regrettably his chance to prove himself further came at the very decade when both the English theatre and the movie industry were more interested in stars than in the role of drama and film in English-language cultures. His success, courtesy of Shakespeare and Hollywood, was as a star and not as a member of either a national repertory company or some new artistic or intellectual wave. Olivier too had become a star and one just as proud of his individual talent but he had been brought up within a metropolitan tradition of theatre and when tradition promised to change he was well pleased both to join and then control new developments .

To contemplate the comparison with Olivier, an actor whose brilliance he had momentarily equalled, is to realise how fully Richard Burton owed so many of his qualities and flaws to the time and place of his upbringing. He had been encouraged by his own awareness of his gifts and by the ambitions of his mentor to aim for the highest prizes within certain English cultural traditions. The prizes had been gained but he had won them as an outsider. He had won victories on deeply respected but nevertheless alien territory. He had not attempted to integrate into any new culture or to submit himself to any new disciplines and codes of conduct. The English and Americans could swoon at his voice, his 'stillness' and his beauty but they could not lay claim to a personality that was already quite sure of itself and which received all the acclaim and reassurance that it needed from a society with a very different set of values. Stratford and Broadway could claim him as a natural prince but his royal credentials, his sense of being special and his sense of being clever had all been established in a different society whose approval he respected more. England and America wanted him as an actor who would work within their dramatic and cinematic traditions but Burton himself had already been encouraged by the traditions of his own society with its thirst for education, for literature and for social justice to believe that his rather physical success as an actor could be used as the launching-pad for a career of even wider significance. He knew so much about the miners, about South Wales, about Anglo-Welsh writing and story-telling that it could only be as a writer or indeed as a politician that he believed he could do justice to what he had been born as and to what he had been made into. Everything about him would seem to argue for him being special in this broader sense and yet the only time when true distinction had been achieved had been that very sudden and relatively short-lived period on the English stage from which he had so quickly gone into exile.

The tragedy of Burton's life was to be the tragedy of exile. Whatever the financial logic of that exile it was always an experience that he was able to endure because he could take so many things with him. His family, his Welshness, his story-telling could all be celebrated as he enjoyed the fruits of his wealth. It was an exile though that cut him off from a Wales and a Britain that were dramatically smashing class barriers and greatly enriching their cultural traditions. His own career was no longer one aspect of how a working-class society had striven to produce its own heroes but rather he now stood outside History and necessarily had to create his own frame of reference. London with its great theatres was the only place that could bestow further distinction to his reputation and he loved the notion that one day he would return as Sir Richard. But there was always a fear of the place and a rejection of it. Any return would involve massive compromises and sacrifices not least in respect of the only sure sense he had of himself. He willingly became Mr Elizabeth Taylor and made a career of being married to her because there was something about her that took him back to the relatives with whom he had grown up. With her too he became indeed the figure of world importance that he felt himself to be. This was the confirmation of being special and of being royal that he really wanted. And yet all the while he could reassure himself that he remained an Anglo-Welsh intellectual.

For all his story-telling he was essentially a serious man for whom life had been full of very real tragedies. It has been suggested that all his yarns and all his merriment were in part a disguise for his loneliness and his guilt. Very early on Caryl Brahms had instantly spotted that lack of a sunny disposition, that 'curdled' quality, that melancholy that really made him a limited film actor, and one who could never have received the international affection that was bestowed on two other British stars from working-class backgrounds, Sean Connery and Michael Caine. Perhaps there were times too when he was aware that even that Anglo-Welsh literary and scholarly identity to which he clung and to which he looked for development was not enough. Certainly the only comic rôle in which he ever looked fully at home was that of the drunken hymn-spouting Welsh poet, 'the bloody Welshman', in *Candy*, and here he was really parodying everything that he had always held to be important. At all other times he was yearning and striving for deep significance and for consolation, not fully aware that his visionary eyes, his stillness and his majestic voice had only really been given meaning by Shakespeare. Without the bard they were empty things, and for all the temporary pleasure that they could bring in bars and restaurants and when making love, there was a need for something more. "Twenty years ago I would have been in a pulpit" he could flippantly remark but he knew that to be very true. The stage and perhaps adult life in general had been something of a disappointment. The promise of a very special youth needs careful training before it can flourish as an adult skill and what especially has to be learnt is a sense of ignorance and then of proportion. It was the fate of Richard Burton, who was for a while possibly the greatest Shakespearean actor in the English-speaking world, to be granted instant wealth and fame by the exercise of a talent of which he was enormously proud but never fully understood. In respect of that talent he had immediately assumed that there was nothing more to learn, that it could be taken for granted even as it was used to launch a wider fame. Eventually he was trapped by his own vanity and innocence, aspects of his personality that had been fostered by a Wales hungry for success and by an England and America longing for new talent but not wanting to pay any social or intellectual price for it.

Select Bibliography

On Richard Burton

Hollis Alpert, Burton (1986)

Melvyn Bragg, *Richard Burton, A Life* (1988)

Fergus Cashin, *Richard Burton* (1982)

John Cottrell & Fergus Cashin, *Richard Burton* (1971)

Paul Ferris, *Richard Burton* (1981)

Paul Ferris, *A Portrait of Richard Burton* (1984)

Graham Jenkins, *Richard Burton, My Brother* (1988)

Penny Junor, *Burton, The Man Behind the Myth* (1985)

Ruth Waterbury, *Richard Burton, His Intimate Story* (1965)

Material Cited

Philip Burton, *Granton Street* (1934)

Philip Burton, *Early Doors, My Life and the Theatre* (1969)

Richard Burton, *A Christmas Story* (1965)

Richard Burton, *Meeting Mrs Jenkins* (1965)

Richard Burton, 'The last time I played rugby' (*The Observer*, 4 October, 1970)

Richard Burton, 'Lament for a dead Welshman' (*ibid.*, 11 July 1976)

Essays on Burton

Anthony Burgess, 'Richard Burton, Prince of Players' (*The Washington Post*, 22 January, 1989)

Hal Burton (ed.), *Acting in the Sixties* (1970)

Ethan Mordden, *The Fireside Companion to the Theatre* (1988)

Sheridan Morley, *The Great Stage Stars* (1986)

David Shipman, *The Great Movie Stars* (1980 edn.)

Andreas Teuber, 'Harvard Grad. to Act with Burton', (*Harvard Alumni Bulletin*, 1969)

David Thomson, *A Bibliographical Dictionary of the Cinema* (1975)

Peter Thomson & Gamini Salgado, *The Everyman Companion to the Theatre* (1985)

Alan Watkins, 'Would You Sincerely Like to be Rich?' (*The Spectator*, 8 October, 1988)

On the Stage

Brooks Atkinson, *Broadway* (1974)
Judith Cook (ed), *Shakespeare's Players* (1983)
John Elsom, *Post-War British Theatre Criticism* (1981)
Walter Kerr, *Journey to the Centre of the Theatre* (1979)
William Redfield, *Letters From An Actor* (1967)
Peter Roberts (ed.), *The Best of Plays and Players 1953-1968* (1988)
Peter Roberts, *The Old Vic Story* (1976)
J.C. Trewin, *Five and Eighty Hamlets*, (1987)
Kenneth Tynan, *A View of the English Stage* (1975)
Audrey Williamson, *Contemporary Theatre* (1956)
T.C. Worsley, *The Fugitive Art* (1952)

On the Screen

Roy Armes, *A Critical History of British Cinema* (1978)
Peter Bogdanovich, *Picture Shows* (1975)
Manny Farber, *Negative Space* (1971)
Mel Gussow, *Don't Say Yes Until I Finish Talking* (1971)
Leonard Mosley, *Zanuck* (1985)
Jay Scott, *Midnight Matinees* (1985)
Alexander Walker, *National Heroes* (1985)
Alexander Walker, *It's Only a Movie, Ingrid* (1988)
Maurice Yacowar, *Tennesee Williams and Film* (1977)

Biographical Themes

Melvyn Bragg, *Laurence Olivier* (1989 edn)
Quentin Falk, *Anthony Hopkins, Too Good to Waste* (1989)
Richard Findlater, *Emlyn Williams* (1956)
John Gielgud, *An Actor and His Time* (1979)
Richard Huggett, *Binkie Beaumont* (1989)
Brenda Maddox, *Who's Afraid of Elizabeth Taylor?* (1977)
Peter Noble, *Ivor Novello* (1951)
Laurence Olivier, *On Acting* (1986)
Michael Redgrave, *In My Mind's I* (1983)
Alun Richards, *Carwyn* (1984)
Anthony Storey, *Stanley Baker, Portrait of an Actor* (1977)

Index

Performance Index